Dear N

Hope this book is
of interest + value 4 you

Paul

VISION

The Search for a Spiritual Pathway

by
Paul H. Skinner, Ph.D.
with
Valerie A. Skinner, M.Ed.

VISION: *The Search for a Spiritual Pathway*

Publisher:
Friends of Spirituality, Healing, and Health
1642 E. Helen Street
Tucson, AZ 85719

This publication is designed to provide accurate and authoritative information in regard to the subject matter covered. It is sold with the understanding that the publisher and author are not engaged in rendering counseling, psychological, medical, or other professional services. If expert assistance or counseling is needed, the services of a competent professional should be sought.

Library of Congress Cataloging-in-Publication Data

Skinner, Paul H.
    Vision : the search for a spiritual pathway /
by Paul H. Skinner ; with Valerie A. Skinner. –
1st ed.
    p.   cm.
    Includes bibliographical references and index.
    LCCN: 99-91582
    ISBN: 0-9676591-0-8

    1. Spiritual life. 2. Self-actualization
(Psychology)–Religious aspects.   3. Spiritual
healing.   I. Skinner, Valerie A.   II. Title.
BL624. S55 2000   291.4
                    QB199-1731

*Cover and Book Design by Sharon Nicks, Types
Logo Graphic Design by Leslie Johnston*

ACKNOWLEDGMENTS

To my teachers, and to my students who are also my teachers; And to each of you who shares the experience of this book.

Thanks to my colleagues, Dr. Robert Young and Dr. Jeanette Hassin, for their editorial support and contributions, and to my teaching assistants, Ms. Monika Czerski and Mr. Chris Lovato. A special note of thanks to my associate, Ms. Jana Rivera, for her editorial assistance.

To my father, Edgar G. Skinner, who introduced me to critical thinking.

And to my wife, Valerie, for her support and contributions in this work through our interpersonal communication and our life process.

TABLE OF CONTENTS

INTRODUCTION

It Would Take a Miracle

When my wife, Valerie, and I first heard about mental and spiritual healing, we were unimpressed; it sounded superficial to us. Valerie was suffering from a degenerative, congenital hip dysplasia (a poorly developed hip joint), although we didn't know it at the time because we were told simply that she had arthritis of the hip. We didn't realize the term *arthritis* has different meanings to different specialists. We had heard from many sources that arthritis is often *curable*, and we were seeking every conceivable way to *cure* it.

Valerie was in pain and limping badly. We were desperately searching for natural and even supernatural healing for her, given that her other alternative was to receive an artificial hip through major surgery.

We searched for a cure through conventional medicine, prescription drugs, herbs, diet, fasting, acupressure, massage, and manipulative therapy. We tried programs such as "Science of Mind," (Holmes) and "Attitudinal Healing" (Jampolsky). We explored faith and spiritual healing, and we became students of *A Course in Miracles*, astounding "channeled" material published in 1976 by the Foundation for Inner Peace. You name it, we tried it!

Devoted friends, including physicians, all told us that Valerie was foolish to endure this searching and experimenting. "Just have the surgery," they said. "Stop this anguish and strife." Indeed, they were right given Valerie's condition. Little did they know, however, nor did we fully understand ourselves, that our search was for something beyond a cure. We were searching for a key to true healing. Ironically, we did not really know what healing meant, much less understand the process. Yet we had come to embrace holistic ideas about our health and healing, including a *new age* belief that we cause, and thus can cure, our own illness and disease.

We were not interested in attitudinal healing or *feel good* therapy, which to us meant acceptance of the problem. We wanted a way to *heal* the body directly, a physical cure. That's what healing meant to us. After all, we were new age people; we were going to conquer disease.

During this process, Valerie did not suffer alone, for I also experienced mental anguish. Valerie frequently felt that my attitude was not supportive, and I frequently felt that Valerie's attitude was not conducive to healing. Embroiled in our own doubts and fears, we often got upset and blamed each other for what we were experiencing. But we were not interested in mental and spiritual healing. We wanted a physical cure! So when all else failed, we resigned ourselves, apparently without a choice, to surgery. Thus, we endured the anguish and fear that we felt, because no natural healing seemed possible.

Not unrelated to our mental anguish was the fact that our relationship had never been one of mutual acceptance and support. Although we were quite successful by society's standards, our personal relationship was lacking. I was hypercritical and reactive even about things beyond Valerie's control. Consequently, Valerie had developed a deep and growing resentment and harbored numerous cherished grievances toward me.

The barriers in our relationship seemed as real to us as any physical condition. What hope was there for healing in a relationship so pervaded by guilt? Nevertheless, we remained unimpressed with mental and spiritual healing; we thought the problems we had were physical, for we had proof in our experience.

Even so, we both somehow realized deep within that our suffering was not just about Valerie's hip. Our suffering was really a result of how we felt about ourselves and each other. Although we never clearly understood it or even brought it to awareness, we realized that if our relationship had been complete in mutual acceptance, free of guilt, and fully loving, we could have resolved any matter of life or death and supported each other.

We gradually became aware that mental and spiritual healing was not superficial; indeed, it was profound! This was the beginning for us of something that transcends a physical cure; this was the beginning of true healing. We had pursued practically every external source, only to discover that true healing is a process from within. We also realized that the first step to Valerie's physical healing was to heal ourselves and our relationship with each other.

Valerie's surgery was successful, and x-rays later demonstrated an intact bone graft and artificial joint. The treatment was successful; however, the healing was yet to be done. Valerie had to learn how to use the artificial joint – she had to learn to walk again. It became clear to both of us as she continued to limp that with or without a new hip, the success of her treatment depended on mental and spiritual healing. She could relearn to walk normally or surrender hopelessly and perhaps even in time defeat the success of the surgery. It came down to attitude, the last as well as the first step in true healing.

Although I had no apparent serious physical problems, I was also in need of healing; my anguish and fear were renewed because Valerie was not responding to treatment. I continued to react with guilt and fear, which I projected unconsciously to Valerie. She in turn, perceiving attack, counterattacked, and the cycle continued. It became painfully clear that our problem was no longer physical but purely mental and spiritual.

We became intrigued and began to investigate the process of mental and spiritual healing. We were astounded by countless stories of self-healing and healing relationships that led not only to the restoration of inner peace and happiness, but also to the release of body symptoms and diseases.

Let me share some anecdotes about the benefits of mental and spiritual healing. A friend was having serious problems with a daughter who was using drugs. The mother was constantly upset about her daughter and suffered erratic periods of hypertension (high blood pressure) and tachycardia (spells of rapid heart beat). Through personal healing, she changed her perceptions about her daughter, and soon she discovered, to her surprise, that her hypertension and tachycardia had disappeared.

In another situation, a young woman I know suffered from migraine headaches so severely that she occasionally ruptured blood vessels in her eyes and often wore a patch over one eye or the other. She had experienced bitterness and rejection for years because her parents divorced and both abandoned her, but through self-healing, her migraine attacks gradually disappeared.

Two friends of ours were diagnosed, each by several neurologists, as having ALS (Lou Gehrig's disease), which is described in neurology texts as always fatal. Both were told they were living on "borrowed time." One of our friends slowly degenerated hopelessly and died. The other, Evy, who was a professional nurse, was told she would die within the year. We saw Evy in June of that year, and she was practically helpless in a wheelchair. More or less in desperation, she joined a small commune of people who were ruthlessly honest, but open, loving, and supportive. They told her she could do as she pleased, live or die, and they would accept her decision. With their support, Evy completely changed her attitude about herself. She celebrated her "death day" in the fall of the year at the time of her predicted death, and by the end of the year she was even walking. Now Evy is traveling nationally to share her healing experience.

The need for mental and spiritual healing is manifested in countless ways through anti-social and anti-personal behaviors such as substance abuse, and through mind-body diseases. That the type-A personality is a candidate for heart disease is common knowledge, as are the effects of psychological stress in diabetes, and it is widely recognized that cancer and heart disease are very often preceded by loss and prolonged depression. Numerous experiences of spontaneous symptom remission (physical healing) have been reported and documented through mental and spiritual healing (O'Regan and Hirshberg). Mental and spiritual healing is a powerful force – a choice available to each one of us.

Once Valerie and I had begun our search, there was no turning back. We found ourselves on an inevitable pathway, and everything in our past now clearly appeared as part of our preparation. We became inspired students and teachers. I became rejuvenated in my study of science as old data took on new meaning.

Our search for healing became our purpose, like a predetermined commitment we made "out of time." Indeed, it became our life process, for we had several of the most fundamental lessons to be learned. There is no more effective way to learn than through experience, and we had to do our learning the hard way.

More than a year had passed since Valerie's hip surgery, and she still was not walking normally. The treatment was a technical success, yet healing had not been accomplished. After the surgery and the limitations of an artificial hip, Valerie experienced a deep sense of loss, personal upsets, and profound depression and apathy, which was apparent to those closest to her.

Before Valerie's hip problem and surgery, she was a marvel of energy and activity. Although her physical and mental decline had been protracted and gradual, I was disheartened by the change. Moreover, I was afraid that Valerie might never walk normally again, and worse, afraid that Valerie wasn't really trying. Clearly what was missing was the key ingredient: mental and spiritual healing.

In close relationships, when one person is not at peace, others involved often join in the suffering. Each unconsciously may become a victim, and both parties feel guilty. Although the situation is experienced unconsciously, the message is clear: "at your hands I suffer."

In our experience, there were many times when we reinforced each other's guilt, fear, and sickness, often unknowingly and even with good intentions. We pointed out the other's need for correction, for we saw each other through the eyes of sickness. Our interactions became a series of perceived attacks, and counterattacks. They were a part of our sickness, not a part of healing.

About a year later, Valerie started to experience backaches and pain, and we suspected it was related to improper walking. This proved to be the beginning of an almost unbearable crisis. Valerie, now in severe pain, agreed to gall bladder surgery recommended by both a confident internist and a surgeon, which unfortunately was based on a false diagnosis. Subsequent to the surgery, her pain became even more intense, and numerous visits to physicians and hospitals led to more false diagnoses, incomplete examinations, and assurances that she was "healthy as a horse." Her pain was diagnosed as psychological because no physical basis for her pain was detected. All of this occurred over weeks and weeks of excruciating pain, sleepless nights, fear, despair, and emotional trauma.

Then came the crisis. Valerie's body went numb from the waist down, and she began to stumble and soon was unable to walk. We returned to the hospital immediately and received a new series of diagnoses, confounded by previous false ones. Finally came the discovery: a massive malignant tumor had encompassed her thoracic spine. Emergency surgery was performed after which I was told that Valerie only had two or three weeks to live.

As the trauma and shock subsided, our lives seemed to unravel before us. A friend remarked, "There is nothing like cancer to slap you into reality."

Valerie and I confronted almost overwhelming emotional experiences of past grievances, anguish, and guilt, which led to spontaneous releases: from grief and sorrow to forgiveness and love. It was quite literally a miraculous experience. We confronted in our lives the truth about what really matters: forgiveness, love, and relationships. We started to gain a new perspective about life. Ironically, in the midst of our experience of cancer and pending death, we knew intuitively that we had discovered true healing! We realized that the key to our healing was to rediscover each other in forgiveness and love. In doing so, I realized that Valerie was healed despite the symptoms of her body. I realized as well that I was healed myself, for I no longer saw Valerie in sickness. In turn, Valerie was able to re-experience me and our relationship through forgiveness and love, which was also the key to her healing. As we shared our thoughts and our experiences with each other, the miracle of healing became a mutually shared experience.

Mental and spiritual healing is simple in principle, but it

is not an easy process. It is not simply positive thinking. Healing requires a personal transformation. Changing the mind is a miracle that can restore inner peace and happiness regardless of life situations, and healing the mind may or may not release bodily symptoms and diseases. This is the process of healing, a reversal of how we usually think. Communication is the key to changing the mind, to forgiveness and healing, and to the rediscovery of oneness, love, and inner perfection.

The medical prognosis was grave. Valerie was now confined to a wheelchair with loss of sensation and control from her waist down. We were informed by her physicians that she may never walk again, and this she had to confront (and live with) in the face of an even more dire prediction. Despite the two to three week death prediction of her physicians, Valerie did not agree to die, and she vowed that she would walk again. A friend referred us to a Christian Science practitioner. Through the practitioner's conviction and support, we began our goal toward inner healing. Valerie became inspired and empowered. Another friend recommended an oncologist, and he brought us new hope and encouragement through medical treatment. Valerie started intense physical therapy in an effort to regain control of her paralyzed lower body, and she also adopted a macrobiotic diet recommended by Dr. Andrew Weil, who was a controversial physician in the Tucson community. Dr. Weil offered needed encouragement, breathing exercises, vitamin and herbal therapy, as well as high expectations for Valerie's recovery. As a result of much needed assistance, Valerie regained her former enthusiasm and made a commitment to full recovery. She not only survived her acute state of cancer, but she gradually regained control of her legs, and after many months she was able to walk normally again. Valerie received lots of help in her recovery; however, it is absolutely clear to us that mental and spiritual healing was the key to her choice for recovery.

We had learned the hard way through experience that symptoms and treatment are manifested in the body, but true healing is of the mind and spirit. We experienced healing within by changing our minds, by a miraculous shift in perception. We continue to have many challenging lessons. Healing is a journey, not a destination. We continue to make mistakes and to learn and grow, but our lives will never be the same. We have learned how to release suffering and despair and to live with inspiration and gratitude. And we teach and we share what we need to learn.

CHAPTER ONE

What You Choose Is What You Get
What's So

It often looks like our experience of life more or less happens to us. Your spouse or friend is in a bad mood and says something that hurts your feelings. A waitress is rude to you. You may be unhappy at work. A driver in the car near to you does something that threatens your safety. And often we experience rejection in our relationships or disappointments in the behavior of others. Frequently things do not happen the way we want them to. We know from past experience that miscommunication, upsets, and suffering are facts of life. "Let's be realistic," we say. "Life is a painful experience!" That is reality, and there seems to be little we can do about it. Often we are left feeling impotent and powerless in our pursuit of life. We have more or less unconsciously come to accept such a conclusion about life, and we seem to have the proof in our experience. Indeed, such is the experience of unconscious perception and what we think about reality.

When we perceive life unconsciously, we don't realize that we have a choice in how we experience life. Without awareness, we relinquish our power of choice, which is ultimately our only real power. To rediscover and regain our power, we must consciously look at how we perceive and communicate, for this process determines our personal reality. Learning and growing can be painful as well as exhilarating; in either case, it takes courage and integrity to examine the process. Yet this is the way to rediscover freedom and personal power: the power of choice! If you choose, you can discover a new reality.

The first step is to discover what is meant by reality and to discover how reality unfolds (Arndt). Notice that an inner voice may comment at this point, "Oh great – here we go again, another philosophical trip." However, allow me to remind you that perception and reality are very practical matters.

Reality

Reality – what a concept. — Robin Williams

Reality is simply what's so. But what's so for whom? Who gets to say what's so? Scientists tell us that reality is the natural state of the universe, the reality of nature. They also tell us that we can perceive only a fraction of what exists in the universe. Thus, each answer about reality leads to a new question. Scientists are continually trying to understand and describe what's so: gravity, relativity, quantum mechanics, personality, being, communication. Will we ever know?

The problem is that reality cannot be found externally (outside us) because we "create" our own reality by how we choose to think. Physicists insist that the material world is reality, and yet they say that matter is made of inert (lifeless) particles. Some physicists propose theories of everything but do not include life in their theories. Many biologists and physicians believe that the body is the source of life and of our reality. Many psychologists believe that the mind is the source of reality; and mystics, ministers, and people in general insist that spirit is reality. In fact, researchers are seeking scientific evidence to support these ideas (Tart). I conclude that thought or mind – how we think – is the source of our reality. What do you think? Take your choice!

Personal Reality

Because no human being knows what's so, we rely on our perception to seek understanding. Scientists are not the only ones who interpret reality. We all do it. Each of us is a philosopher whether we know it or not! We all have our own perceptions, experiences, and beliefs about reality, and for each one of us that is what's so. Every individual has his or her own personal reality, and for that person that reality is absolutely the way it is – if he or she says so. Why? Because he or she *created it that way* through personal perception, experience, and belief.

> *Awareness is the first step to a healthier life. It is a mental stretching that limbers up your perceptions, making you loose enough to let go and thus allowing an element of creative choice to enter your experience.*   — Joan Borysenko

Our interpretation becomes our reality, and because each of us has our own unique set of perceptions, attitudes, experiences, and beliefs, each of us creates our own unique reality. Just as surely as we will agree on certain aspects of the real world, we will have disagreements about other aspects. The problem in communication is that rather than me understanding your reality and you understanding my reality, each of us will argue that our own reality is correct! It is like the elephant poem:

Six wise men of India
An elephant did find
And carefully they felt its shape
(For all of them were blind).

The first he felt towards the tusk,
'It does to me appear,
This marvel of an elephant
Is very like a spear.'

The second sensed the creature's side
Extended flat and tall,
'Ahah!' he cried and did conclude,
'This animal's a wall.'

The third had reached towards a leg
And said, 'It's clear to me
What we should all have instead
This creature's like a tree.'

The fourth had come upon the trunk
Which he did seize and shake,
Quoth he, 'This so-called elephant
Is really just a snake.'

The fifth had felt the creature's ear
And fingers o'er it ran,
'I have the answer, never fear,
The creature's like a fan!'

The sixth had come upon the tail
As blindly he did grope,
'Let my conviction now prevail
This creature's like a rope.'

And so these men of missing sight
Each argued loud and long
Though each was partly in the right
They all were in the wrong.

— Anonymous

In other words, your reality is true for you, although not necessarily "the truth," even though you may think it is. The problem is that we usually fail to distinguish between what we think and what is the truth. How can I tell who or what is right? Let me share a story with you to help clarify this.

Who Says So?

Who says so? Let's say that I know that I am Napoleon

reincarnated. Because I truly believe this and have a Napoleon hat and coat, and I stand with my arm tucked inside, I even have the proof. This is true for me; it is my reality. As you might suspect, a rather sizable group of detractors insist I am not Napoleon. They claim they have proof because they voted, and all agreed I am an impostor.

And so you see, there is still another reality – no, not the one I share with Napoleon, but reality based upon agreement. And if you don't think agreement is reality, insist you also are Napoleon and see what happens. You can see there is no end to realities. Each of us has our own personal reality, and groups who agree on their own interpretations have group realities. There are groups who agree on social, religious, and political realities. Many people have organized to establish and promote various religious realities, that is, individuals who agree their beliefs are an accurate description of reality. Indeed, their beliefs are what's so for them because they believe them, and each group can prove that its reality is the truth. As you can see, more elephant stories. A lot of insane things happen in the name of God and righteousness when people insist their reality is what's so and judge and condemn others for having a different reality. The history of inquisitions and religious and political wars might make us wonder about who is really sane and who is not. Choose what works, what is right for you, but realize that your choice is not a license to judge others or to determine what they should believe.

Society's definition of reality usually is based on agreed-upon values, morals, and living standards. A colleague of mine (Williams) described our society's metaphors for reality as money, power, and speed: "Grab all the gusto you can get." I didn't say society's definition was good or bad, it's just agreement about what's so for many people.

> *"I know wot's wot!" said a scoundrel to Long John*
> *Silver, who in turn replied,*
> *"Ah it's a wise man as knows that."*
> — Film adaptation of R.L. Stevenson's
> *Treasure Island*

We cannot ignore the influence of parents, teachers, and society in shaping our personal reality, and each of our individual realities is constantly programmed by mass communication (e.g., newspapers and television). Look at your personal reality and see what is so for you. Reality by agreement is merely "wot's wot," but it usually is not what's so. Thus, you can readily see that your reality is shaped by your values, perceptions, and beliefs, and how you think is shaped by your reality.

If an individual is taught and accepts that society's reality is real-reality, then that is so for the individual. For example, there is a book that tells you how to name your child and how to groom "*it*" and rear "*it*" for the right prep school. All of us, more or less, have bought into society's reality in bits and pieces, and many have bought into it lock, stock, and barrel! After all, what will people think if we don't buy into society's definition of reality? A humorist once said, "Don't worry about what people think, so very few really do."

So here we are, stuck in our realities: 1) real reality, what's so; 2) your personal reality, what's so for you, what you insist is the real world, where I wonder about you and you wonder about me; and 3) reality by agreement: what groups agree to call reality. For example, society agreed that the world was flat and later agreed it was round.

What's So For You

Silence your inner voice or thinking. If you can do this successfully, you will notice that all your inner communication stopped. Now free your mind and just be. You will discover that to resume communication with yourself or others, you must resume thinking. Thoughts are the source of our perception and communication whether expressed silently or aloud.

Practicing silence means making a commitment to take a certain amount of time to simply BE.
— Deepak Chopra

Mental Reality

Our thoughts become our reality. In fact, your thoughts are absolutely real for you on the mental level. Whatever you think or believe is your mental reality. Our thoughts give meaning to everything we see. In fact, our thoughts determine our reality because they determine how we perceive and experience what we call reality. Eastern philosophy tells us that the physical world is an illusion because it has only the reality we give it by our thoughts. We can change our reality in every situation by changing our mind – by changing how we think!

I am reminded of the death of my father-in-law who had

suffered from a stroke and became unable to communicate. Subsequently, he became senile and very hostile. Nursing homes refused to have him, and his wife became a nervous wreck trying to take care of him. He was living a miserable existence. When he died of a second stroke, his family experienced his death as relief and a blessing. Ironically, his closest friend, who had been his fishing buddy from childhood, wept like a child over the loss of his friend.

Emotional Reality

Notice also that all your emotions start with thought. This can be difficult to see because thoughts and perceptions are often unconscious, and the first things we actually notice are our feelings. Thus, we may falsely conclude that our feelings and experiences just happen to us. To change your emotional reality, you must change your thoughts, in other words, change your mind. Once again, clear your mind of all thoughts and see if you can create an emotion. Need I point out how difficult it is to quiet or clear your mind of thoughts for longer than a brief period? That is why people who are learning to meditate use a mantra. A mantra is a verse or expression that you repeat silently over and over again. In repeating a mantra, we block out random and distracting thoughts that continually float through our minds.

Thought is a habit. — Alfred Korzybski

Notice how conditioned your thoughts and emotions become. We seem to have little control over them. It takes training, discipline, and strong inner desire or will (spirituality) to change or release our programmed thoughts and our emotional reality.

Physical Reality

Notice that your conscious action or behavior starts with thought. Try to initiate voluntary behavior in the absence of thought. In fact, psychologists and healers have shown that people can regulate or modify so-called involuntary action through conscious thought. In controlled laboratory experiments, certain people were able to regulate their own heart beat and stop and start blood flow from an incision in their body (*Biofeedback: Yoga of the West*). One may reasonably speculate that all bodily action can be started, modified, or stopped by conscious thought. Once consciously or unconsciously activated, the mind's program will continue indefinitely until the on-going action is recognized and consciously stopped. Voluntary action, at the very least, must start at the level of thought, and this action becomes one's physical reality.

What Is Reality?

In summary, an individual's reality is initiated by thought 1) on the mental plane; 2) which leads to emotions on the feeling plane; indeed, all feelings and sensations are either created, interpreted, or given meaning through thought; which 3) leads to action on the physical plane.

Thought and mental action are the creative force or energy behind all things manifested on the emotional and physical planes and the determination of what we call reality. It looks to us that what we call real reality, the world around us – what we call the real world – causes our thoughts, feelings, and behaviors. Yet our personal reality is our interpretation of real reality.

I am reminded of a joke about kamikaze pilots. A Japanese kamikaze squadron commander was giving last minute instructions to his men. He told them to crash their bomb-laden planes into vulnerable places on American aircraft carriers. At the end of the briefing, the commander asked, "Are there any questions?" A wide-eyed pilot rose from the group. "I have one question," he said in alarm. "Are you out of your mind?!!"

The result of such action in physical reality, of course, is that the pilots and planes would be blown to bits. That is what's so. These are the laws of physical reality apparently unchangeable by our minds. There is as well an individual or personal reality – your reality – which is what is so for you under given circumstances. You may not be able to change the circumstances, but you can interpret them as you choose.

Thus, each individual kamikaze pilot's creation of his experience becomes his personal reality! Imagine the squadron diving in formation to crash their planes into a ship. The first pilot says to himself, "What an opportunity. I will glorify myself and my country." He is thrilled! The second says to himself, "How do I get out of this Mickey Mouse outfit?" The third is a miserable victim. "It's all my father's fault. I never wanted to be a pilot anyhow. He made me do it." A fourth may be thinking, "I am scared to death to do this, but if I back out, what will people think?"

Your personal reality is your creation, so what you create

is what you get. You may have no control over real reality, but you have full control over your interpretation of it. You create it all through your thoughts and perceptions. When you can't control the physical circumstances, the only choice is to choose how you experience the situation. This is it and I love it, or this is it and I hate it. Problem or opportunity, it's your choice.

Cause And Effect...Effect...Effect...Effect

I know that it is an awfully heavy trip to say you cause your own personal reality. I often squirm under my own. But if you are angry, happy, upset, or joyful, who says so? If you recognize that you cause your own reality, then you have a choice about how you experience it. Most of what looks to us to be caused by real reality is actually caused by our thoughts and perceptions. People often make themselves ill, alcoholic, miserable, rich, or poor, yet they are unaware – not conscious – that they did it. If we acknowledge that we create our personal reality, then we can choose how we experience it.

If our interpretation is that we are victims of circumstance – "the world did it to me," "God did it to me," or "the devil made me do it," as comedian Flip Wilson says – then we are the effect of what happens. We then deny we created our personal reality; someone else forced it on us, they made us do it, etc., etc., etc., effect, effect, effect.

If you believe that feelings and experiences just happen to you, and you take the bad with the good, that's your choice. You will be the victim of much of your perception, communication, and relationships. If you choose to experience yourself as cause and creator of your perception and communication, then you can transform your relationships and personal reality. It's up to you. You have a choice.

Projection: You may think that someone out there causes your experience. For example, "Joe made me angry," you tell yourself. Obviously, Joe did or said what he did, and your perception verifies that. You may even have further proof: Joe may even admit he did it. Thus, the obvious conclusion is that Joe made you angry or Joe upset you. This is what psychologists call projection. Joe does something to which you react. Yet your reaction is your creation and no one else's. You created your own reaction, but your perception tells you that Joe caused it; Joe did it to you. By blaming Joe, you deny the responsibility for your own creations.

Dissociation: You assign your behavior and the cause of it to an external person or source and dissociate yourself from the source, the act, and the cause. Joe caused it; he is the cause, which is separate from you. You dissociate yourself from the true cause (your thoughts and perceptions) and project the cause onto Joe. Projection and dissociation lead you to create a false cause for your own behavior. The problem is that you lose the power over your behavior, making it appear that you are the effect of your personal reality rather than the cause of it. The more responsibility you project (that is, assign false cause to others), the less control you have over your own perception and behavior.

An excellent analogy is a moving picture projector. The film or tape is fed into the projector in the same way that our senses perceive or communicate with the world around us. The input (images) to the projector is reflected by light beams onto a screen. Our eyes and perception will tell us the images we see are coming from the screen, yet we know the screen merely reflects what is in the projector. Similarly, images we perceive and the meaning we give to the images come from the mind, yet our perception tells us that what we perceive is something external to us. In this way, the mind creates its own meaning for all of our perceptions, and it projects the cause for that meaning to an external source. In effect, the mind does not see itself as the cause; it does not see that it has created its own reality. We say we believe what we see, but actually we see what we believe, that which we have created in our own minds.

Introjection: The opposite of projection is introjection. Introjection is the belief that you cause the feelings of others. You may tell yourself, for example, to lie about your feelings so that you don't hurt or upset someone else. You can communicate your feelings with integrity and responsibility, however, by knowing that each of us causes our own feelings. Get in touch with your intentions; own your own feelings and communicate responsibly. After all, we create our own feelings.

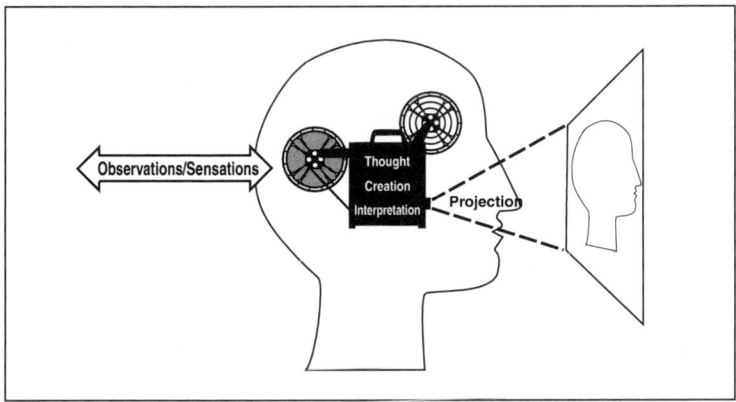

Projection and introjection are based on the belief that the external world is the cause of our feelings.

Let me summarize by an example. I recall a student who said that a boy kept asking her for a date. She made excuses not to go out with him because "he was a loser." (Her interpretation equals her reality.) Several of her friends agreed he was a loser (the proof: reality by social agreement), yet she would not tell him her true feelings in a responsible way. He was "bugging" her (her projection), yet she refused to tell him that she did not want to go out with him because she did not want to hurt his feelings (introjection).

When we operate without full awareness and perceive and behave unconsciously, cause and effect become confused. True cause becomes obscured.

Red Lights And Green Lights

Let's say you just pulled your car up to a red light, and you are waiting for the light to change. Imagine that a car pulls up behind you, and at the instant the light turns green, the driver in the other car blows his horn. What do you do? How do you feel at that instant, and how do you react? Be honest with yourself. You may or may not get annoyed, but people commonly get upset about that sort of thing. One person told me that on one occasion when that happened to her, she purposely hesitated a long time at the green light before driving through the intersection. Another person said that he waited until the light turned yellow and then drove through the intersection, leaving the driver behind him facing a second red light. I know of one situation in which a driver became so angry that he backed his car into the car behind him because that driver was blowing his horn. And I have heard of incidents in which people were even physically assaulted! What would you have done? Let me point out that we aren't considering the facts of the case. Instead, we immediately interpret each situation, and our interpretation becomes real for us. Our experience is as though the facts and our interpretation are one and the same.

Look at the incident again, and this time consider the facts separately from your interpretation. The facts are simple: You were waiting at a stop light, the light turned green, and at the same time the driver in the car behind you blew his horn. That's it. That is the truth, the facts. That's all. How you perceive the incident, how you react, your thoughts, your interpretation – all appearing to be caused by people and events outside you – were all your creation. You decided the car horn was blown at you. That was your experience of the incident. You forgot that you were cause of your interpretation; you believed you were the effect.

Let's say, just to highlight the power of choice in interpretation, that the driver actually blew his horn as he came up to the traffic light to greet a friend on the corner.

We are not aware that we interpret everything we experience because we do so unconsciously. Through our interpretation we give meaning and cause to our perceptions, experiences and life itself.

In reality, we do not see through our eyes or hear through our ears because the meaning we give to our perceptions and experience is created by our minds. We forget that our senses are only the lenses or valves for perception, and that our minds create the meaning. We are so busy interpreting through our thoughts that we rarely observe just the facts. We get only our own interpretations.

Our interpretations involve analysis, judgments, evaluation, and stories, all of which we create with our minds based on our perceptions of the external world, thus cause and effect become confused. Through our interpretations, we may create a false cause and false reality that may seriously impair our well-being, relationships, and our happiness. Look at your everyday experience and distinguish between cause and effect. In doing so, you will experience a new reality.

What You Choose Is What You Get

There's a movement toward things spiritual in general, and a search for wholeness . . . It's as if the void that so many people feel is crying out to be filled, and that the emptiness and rush of modern life is pushing more of us to seek a better and more balanced way.
— Kurt Kaltreider

Your mind forms conclusions – creates your personal reality – unconsciously or consciously from your beliefs and interpretations or your perceptions and experiences. This is the process by which we create our personal reality. If someone asks you how you like the weather, you may look to your senses for information, and then you make a decision: too hot, too cold, just right. You may, however, put aside that sensory input entirely and respond by how you feel about yourself at that moment – not so hot, great, however you feel.

You create your own personal reality. Create a quiet moment. Imagine an experience in which you were very sad. Re-experience that sadness. Imagine an experience in which you became very angry. Re-experience that anger. Imagine an experience in which you were very happy. Recreate that feeling of happiness. Notice that you choose how you recreate those experiences from the past.

Now try to explain how you created each of those experiences and emotions. The dictionary says that a miracle is something that you can't explain by natural laws – a wonder, a marvel. You can create miracles all the time through your own inner communication and your communication with others.

You – your Self – have the potential for creating and experiencing. All you require to actualize that potential is your willingness and intention to do so. And each person has the same potential and ability to create and experience. Your communication can be yours to understand and use for the greatest good or the greatest evil. The power of choice is within you. What you choose is what you get!

Chapter One Insights
What You Choose Is What You Get

1. Discovering Reality
   a. Identify three aspects of physical reality (e.g., light, sound).
   b. Identify three aspects of your personal reality (e.g., belief).
   c. Identify three aspects of reality by agreement (e.g., time).

2. Creating Reality
   Our interpretation of the circumstances and experiences of our lives becomes our personal reality. Look for incidents in which you can discover how this happens. Complete this inventory by giving a meaningful example of a situation for each observation below:
   a. I noticed that when I react to people or situations, I create my own reality.
   b. I noticed that people create different personal realities in observing the same situation.
   c. I noticed that when my interpretation agrees with that of others, our interpretation becomes our reality by agreement.
   d. I noticed that when my interpretation disagrees with that of others, each of us may insist that our own personal reality is right.

3. Cause and Effect
   a. Describe an experience that seemed to *happen* to you, but you now realize that you actually caused yourself (dissociation).
   b. Describe an experience that you caused and then blamed on someone else (projection).
   c. Describe someone else's experience you think you caused (introjection).

CHAPTER TWO

A Meeting With the Creator

Discovering The Source

*Who are you? Where did you come from? Why
are you here? Anyone who can answer those
three questions will be well . . .*
— Lewis Mehl-Madrona

What you perceive is how you feel about yourself. For example, at a party a friend of ours, Carl, who is very tall and quite handsome, bumped into a charming lady. She was quite expressive and said, "Hi, you really look gorgeous up there." Most men would have been flattered, but Carl responded, "I get so tired of people commenting about how things look from up here." Clearly, Carl has some uncomfortable feelings about his height. Those who know Carl are aware that he is self-conscious about his height, and that this self-consciousness is expressed in his posture: he slumps. The lady, whose intentions were so pleasantly flirtatious, became offended because she felt put down by Carl's response, which was simply his feeling about himself.

What we experience is how we feel about ourselves. Recall a time in your life when you were totally satisfied with yourself. It may have been only when you received a brief expression of love, or when you completed a simple task to your standards of perfection. At that moment, you probably also perceived that everyone around you was okay and that the universe was beautiful.

Recall another time when you felt frustrated because you could not achieve a goal or you had failed at a task. What you probably experienced at that moment was dissatisfaction in others and a sense of withdrawal or rejection from the universe. You may have projected your frustrations and anger on someone else. Why didn't your roommate or spouse empty the wastebasket? It was running over! The place is a mess. What's more, you really didn't feel well anyhow.

Sharon was having trouble with a math problem and complained to her mother that math was stupid and, for that matter, so was her math teacher. When her dog playfully jumped on her papers, she pronounced the dog stupid also. In another state, she might experience the dog as playful and loving. Clearly, Sharon was really concerned about herself. In her frustration she may have felt that she was stupid, or that she would indeed appear to be stupid in the eyes of her teacher and others.

You relate to others based on your experience of yourself. It's all so simple, so obvious, and you've always known the truth. Let's look at the source. To do so, we must make certain assumptions about how people operate in communication. I ask you not to accept or reject these assumptions; rather, consider them as hypotheses for you to test and to discover what is true in your communication with others. One suggestion: observe your behavior rather than trying to figure it out.

Assumption One: Our thoughts, beliefs, and experience determine our reality.

We use our beliefs to explain and validate our perceptions, and our perceptions determine our feelings and behavior, our communication, and what we seem to experience. Through communication and experience, we determine what we think we "know," what we call reality. For example, if you believe you can walk, you are willing to learn to do so, and once you have experienced walking, you know you can do it. You also have confirmed your belief, and walking becomes a part of your reality. Since you can walk, you also believe others can walk.

Incredible as it may seem, your beliefs have no limitations. We can believe or not believe anything we choose. And what we believe, we think we know. Beliefs do not require validation by experience or observation. You may believe that someone walked on water even though most of us have never actually observed someone do it. What you choose not to believe simply is not true for you. This self-imposed limitation can greatly restrict one's ability to become self-empowered and to expand one's personal reality.

> *And everyone believes in what he made, for it*
> *was made by his believing it – out of which no*
> *way seems possible.*   — ACIM

In his book, *Actualizations*, Stewart Emery presents the following diagram to depict the above concept.

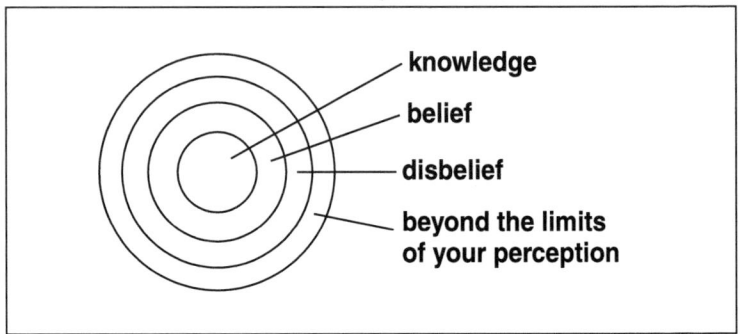

In the center of the circle is knowledge. Knowledge in the strictest sense is that which you have experienced mentally or intuitively as well as physically. In the second circle is belief, that which is believable to you. The third circle is disbelief; anything in this circle is beyond your personal reality and is **by your decision** not real – it is unbelievable to you. In the outermost circle is that which is beyond your perception. Because we commonly use perception as our proof about whether something does or does not exist, we are inclined to doubt what is beyond our ability to perceive.

People usually react to and reject what they don't believe. People are willing to consider and discuss what they do or might believe. If something is outside your experience and knowledge, you probably will respond to it according to whether you find it believable. Is it reasonable by your beliefs, perception, and knowledge?

Let's look at some examples of knowing versus believing. What would your answer be if I asked, "Do you know that scientists and engineers launched a space ship and put a man on the moon?" No doubt you would say, "Yes, of course I know that. I saw it on TV and in the newspapers. Everyone knows that." Now really, do you "know" that? Did you experience that, or is it instead something you believe? What if I told you the whole thing was a Disney production? The point is that you think you know what you believe or don't believe. You don't have to experience something to believe it. You can believe or not believe anything you choose, and your believing it makes it true for you. Can you separate your beliefs from what you know? To know something is to have personally and directly experienced it.

On the other hand, if I said I could levitate or walk on water, you probably would not believe it, even if I demonstrated it for you. You probably would decide that I was a fraud and that somehow I had tricked you. In fact, if I did levitate or walk on water, it might be of no consequence in your life. The point is that you probably would not believe it anyway simply because your beliefs preclude the validity of such a phenomenon. Your beliefs, not the validity of the phenomenon, become the issue.

I once read an article that rigorously proved by the then current laws of physics that it was impossible for flying saucers to visit the planet Earth. The proof at that time appeared valid. Sometime later, however, scientists and engineers sent a man to the moon (so I am told). Often our beliefs limit us rather than expand our ability to discover new experiences. As Richard Bach says:

Argue for your limitations and they will be yours.

Because people have different beliefs and experiences and different interpretations of the same experiences, they also have their own realities. Yet we often argue about one another's reality, invalidate one another's reality, or try to persuade someone to agree with our reality rather than seek to understand what is true for one another. This leads to miscommunication and conflict. History is filled with numerous wars in which each side thought its beliefs were right.

Assumption Two: Each of us is programmed.
There is a story that playwright George Bernard Shaw was highly indignant when Ivan Pavlov, the famous Russian psychologist, received Nobel acclaim for his famous studies about conditioned responses (dogs salivating in response to the sound of a bell, which they were *conditioned*, or *programmed,* to associate with receiving food). Shaw perceived that such conditioned responses or reactions were simply a matter of common knowledge. Such conditioning or programming has been widely studied in experimental psychology and is now recognized to be an inherent part of our lives.

Shaw, in his indignation about Pavlov's recognition, responded with a satire about a young person on a pilgrimage who encountered a snake that suddenly emerged from a tree. Need I describe the person's reaction? I remember a somewhat similar event. While vacationing in the mountains, my wife Valerie called our pet poodle, Willie, to get into the car. Willie jumped in with a tiny mouse in his mouth. While I did not see the mouse, I certainly heard and saw Valerie's reaction because she shouted in alarm and bolted out of the car. Such a situation may be funny to some people, yet it is fearful to others. You may or may not be alarmed by a mouse, but all of us are profoundly conditioned or programmed in many ways.

For example, many university students may be conditioned or programmed to associate fear and stress with examinations. Others may not. I would venture that virtually all persons who are highly experienced in driving in traffic are programmed to stop at a red light. It is now well known that animals and people are extensively conditioned to have physiological or behavioral reactions to countless conditioned stimuli without conscious awareness. In fact, we are all conditioned or programmed to have emotional reactions to our own thoughts or to certain words.

Consider the impact that television has had on our lives. We are not only conditioned by advertisements to buy numerous products we may not really want or need, but we are also conditioned in terms of what we value. We not only are informed about which drugs are best to reduce headaches, but advertisements also quite matter-of-factly assume that drugs are the obvious solution to our headaches and practically all of our bodily symptoms. Similarly, we are being convinced daily about the kind of cars to drive or clothes to wear. I am also convinced that the ever increasing and widespread acts of violence are programmed into our thinking. I am likewise convinced that if we were taught gentle and responsible behavior that violence in our society would decrease. It is a fact that our perception determines our emotions and our behavior.

Our programmed perceptions, emotions, and behaviors are analogous to computer programming. Our computer software packages come in conscious and unconscious programs, but they all are in our "computer" mind. And our brains and bodies perform and respond in many ways much like programmed machines. Our programming is often unpredictable. People behave as rational beings when we are at the level of a conscious program, but we are also inclined to behave irrationally when we are at the level of an unconscious program. Although we explain our unconscious responses and justify our story by our perception of the situation, we often are not fully aware of why we feel or react as we do.

I call this unconsciously conditioned mind, or programming, ego-mind. The "ego" is a self-centered, defensive, and reactive way of thinking. It is programmed to perceive attack and counterattack to protect its self image and identity. We shall discuss the ego-mind more explicitly below. Egocentricity can be seen as a survival mode of perception and behavior that all life forms engage in. Remarkably, we are all unconsciously ego-centrically programmed.

Assumption Three: The ego is a stimulus-response system.

Curiously, the higher the evolution of the life form, the less predictable are the communication patterns. If you walk into a brick wall, the wall's response is fully predictable. If you prick an amoeba, it will predictably withdraw. These are simple stimulus-response systems. If you pet a dog, the dog may lick you or bite you. If you express yourself to a fellow human being, the response is often unpredictable.

Psychologists often seek to explain such unpredictable responses by otherwise sensitive and responsible people as an emergence of conditioned or programmed behavior that

arises through four steps: stimulus-association-generaliza-
tion-response. 1) A "stimulus" is a motivation factor. 2) The
stimulus is "associated" with another factor that gives meaning or significance to the stimulus. 3) The stimulus is "generalized" (associated or related more broadly) to a variety of situations within the conscious or unconscious recollection of the
perceiver. 4) Thus the conditioned stimulus is generalized to
all relevant forms of the original stimulus and all of its potential responses or experiences. Perhaps one can imagine then
the possible behaviors that a conditioned stimulus might
evoke, and why unconsciously conditioned stimuli can lead to
unpredictable responses.

Such S-A-G-R patterns arise quite commonly from the
unconsciously conditioned ego-mind and can lead to devastating modes of behavior. Such modes of behavior can be observed in anyone from time to time. I would suggest that if you
observe your thoughts and behavior very carefully, you will see
such reactions in yourself, and occasionally you may observe
that you are actually acting out such a S-A-G-R pattern of
behavior.

Let us consider a very simple example to clarify the pattern. Imagine yourself as a child in your first week in school.
You want to please your teacher and to have him like you.
However, imagine that you are unconsciously chewing gum,
which is against the rules, and you don't notice it until you
happen to blow a bubble. Your teacher sees you do it. So there
you are standing in the corner in humiliation. All of this happened because of the chewing gum – the *stimulus*.

When you get home you feel depressed and you are too

ashamed to tell your parents what happened, but they are aware something is wrong. Your mother offers you a stick of gum to stimulate you to talk. Suddenly you *associate* the gum with your humiliation, and you review the horrible experience once again in your mind. Now you *generalize* the experience. You feel the humiliation all over again. You think your teacher was cruel. You hate your teacher and yourself. How then do you *respond?* Suddenly you feel ill, too ill to go back to school. You decide to avoid your classmates and your teacher, and not to look at him or say hello. In fact, you decide that you hate school and school teachers, and you are too upset to do your homework. The taste of chewing gum and even looking at the wrapper make you ill.

The human experience of such a S-A-G-R paradigm in communication or behavior is neither obvious nor as simple as the above example. And when our response is triggered by an unconscious S-A-G-R program, we make up an explanation to justify our response, and we end up blaming someone or something else for our behavior. For example, let's say someone says something that hurts your feelings. You immediately, unconsciously, create anger and say, "I am angry because you hurt my feelings." You have justified anger by your hurt feelings, or you justified your response by the explanation you created. Actually, you probably don't know why you are angry. You could have been sad, amused, or disinterested, but you became angry, and justified your anger by an explanation. In other words, your explanation said you had to be angry because your feelings were hurt; you had no choice but to be angry and believe someone else caused it. Watch your S-A-

G-R patterns – you will see them arise time and time again.

Now watch the insane behavior that you see in the world, from anger and depression to sickness, from victimhood to crime, to violence, to wars. All ego behavior is packaged in conditioned programs that are carefully justified and defended.

Look at another example. Let's say someone playfully makes a joke about you. You may also feel playful and laugh about it. Do you say, "I laughed because you teased me"? No, you did not perceive an attack, so you need not make or justify a defense. Then, let's say this person makes another playful joke about you, but this time you get angry. Now you probably need to justify it, and you say, "enough is enough," or "that is not funny." You may not know why you didn't laugh both times or get angry both times. But I promise you, you will justify your response, and you can choose what to believe. Much of our communication is expressed from an unconscious level, an automatic pilot so to speak. It is like driving to work and not remembering the trip, or reading, yet not remembering what you read.

For example, one evening Mary greeted John with, "Let's take Patty to dinner tonight." John was on automatic pilot and responded, "No, we can't afford it." Mary became furious and said, "Patty is one of my dearest friends. She does so many lovely things for me; her husband is out of town, and you are too stingy to even take her to dinner." John said, "Hold it, hold it, please forgive me, I was on automatic pilot. Honestly, I didn't really get your communication. Please call Patty. I would truly love to take her to dinner." Usually when you are on automatic pilot, your response will be protective: "I don't want to." In truth, what you are saying is, "I would rather not be bothered," or "Don't bug me."

Each of us communicates through our own personalized or egocentric stimulus-response system. We may experience a lot of communication in the same way other people do, and when we do, we may agree about that communication. We know it's valid because "everyone agrees," and agreement in communication is reality. We also assuredly experience a lot of communication differently from other people, and when we do, we may disagree with that communication. Nevertheless, your communication programming and experiences are uniquely yours. We often may miss the point, however, that we all do not experience the same communication in a common way.

I recall a meeting when one person there, Fernando, had a major decision that he had to make about his immediate career plans. Several of us agreed to help him resolve his problem, and we rotated around a circle with our questions. The first person, Steve, said, "It's really a matter of money, isn't it?" The next, Jody, said, "You really are enjoying having this problem, aren't you?" Next, Mary Lou said, "Are you confused?" And finally I said, "Are you uncomfortable?" Then Mary Lou said, "Hey, isn't this amazing? Each of us just expressed how we feel about the problem." That is what is true for each of us when we have a problem, but none of us was right about Fernando or about one another.

We process and interpret all the information we receive by our own system. We make up the meaning of the messages we receive and the justification for our responses. Our system is always on automatic pilot, and we may or may not consciously choose how we feel about, or respond to the message. You may or may not be conscious of your response, and for that reason you seem to experience that someone or something else caused it or did it to you.

Experience is a manifestation of who you are and where you are coming from. Your experience is determined by your sensory input, your programming through the mind's recordings of your values, beliefs, perceptions, feelings and experience, and what you think you know, including your social conscience. In short, all of your perceptions, expressions, and communications go through your ego-mind, your personalized filter or process, and thus in many ways truth or reality is different for each one of us. Given such complexity, it is quite remarkable that our communication works at all.

Assumption Four: The ego leads to a false identity.

What is the ego? The answer you get will probably depend on whom you ask. The concept of **ego** has been described in many ways before and after the time of Freud, the individual who is most often associated with the word (Hampden-Turner). I define ego as who you think you are, an identity that you developed out of uncertainty and fear without full awareness. Who am I? Ego is the "you" that you created: a false self. It is your pretense of identity – an image of yourself as separate and different. You may not agree with my use of the term; nevertheless, let's use my definition to account for and describe certain behaviors in communication.

Our egocentricity is a self-serving system: the world rotates around me, and everyone and everything has meaning only in relationship to me. Thus the ego is a stimulus-response system.

The problem is that ego involvement usually causes miscommunication. Notice what happens in your communication and the communication of others when the ego dominates.

We also are subject to social conditioning. "Be a good boy" or "be a nice girl" with their respective injunctions. "Don't cry," or "don't get angry": in short, hide your true feelings. And prejudices exist about wealth, intelligence, race, color, and creed. "You've got to be carefully taught" goes the song about racial prejudice from the 1949 musical, *South Pacific*.

The ego constantly focuses on itself. The birth of ego:

Lucy: "Linus, why do you always carry that blanket?"

Linus: "Because it feels good. Want to try it?"

Lucy hugs the blanket and says, "You are right, Linus, it does feel good."

Then Lucy drapes her head with the blanket and says to Linus, "How do I look?"

Our ego is our mind's distinction of our own individuality. It creates each of us as a separate and self-centered being. Notice that an inner voice may strongly object to this whole definition. Ego identifies you as a person out of its desires, misperceptions, and fear. My ego then becomes my idea of what I want, in which "I" becomes supreme.

*Reliance on ego ultimately leads to more
separation as life becomes a contest and
a competition with designated others.*

— Wayne Dyer

Thus, the ego places itself in competition with any conflicting idea or experience and does its best to prevail. It ruthlessly defends the image it creates and attacks any threat to that image.

*And the devil did grin
for his darling sin
is pride that apes humility.*

— Samuel Taylor Coleridge

Your inner voice may actively reject or question these definitions and assumptions. That is the nature of ego. Your ego may pose as your intellect. Regardless, if you tell the truth and take responsibility for your communication, you will discover that communication does not work if it is egocentric. You undoubtedly have experienced conflict in your communication when you became ego involved or suffered ego attacks.

Assumption Five: Ego manifestation/being right and winning.

The ego is self-righteous and protective. Our images, values, and judgments appear to be right to us, and when we communicate, we try to prove from ego that we are right. If our ego is threatened, we may ruthlessly try to be right and win. If you did not think your beliefs were right, they wouldn't be your beliefs. If the ego's image of itself is threatened, it will save face at all costs. Let someone attack your self-image, concepts, ideas, or beliefs, and observe your reaction as a stimulus-response mechanism.

Notice that whatever goes wrong or disappoints you, you conclude that another person did it to you. It is their fault; someone else is to blame. And if you blow it yourself, if you damage your own ego image, your ego voice will torment you. (Nothing can be more severe with you than your own ego attack upon yourself.) The ego is not inherently known for truth or responsibility. You must look to another part of you, to another way of thinking, to an intuitive voice, to transform your experience. Otherwise, changing your mind's perceptions of events is very difficult. And even if you do change your mind or admit you are wrong (one of ego's least favorite communications), the ego will still make itself right. "Look how good I am: I said I was wrong." The bottom line for ego is being right and winning.

> *I would rather be right than be King.*
> — Oliver Cromwell

Being right does not require that you make someone else wrong. This is an age old truth, yet one that is rarely consciously recognized, given our egocentric conditioning. In his famous book, *How to Win Friends and Influence People*, Dale Carnegie admonished that you cannot make others wrong. Try it and see what happens. Really, purposefully try it! You will discover that it was not the first time you have tried to do so. If you operate out of an egocentric model of reality, then you will try to make the other person wrong for you to be right. You also know from your experience that you can create another model, another reality in which winning and losing transcend a context of right and wrong. You can make your communication work for you if you exercise responsibility and integrity. Be honest with yourself.

I recall a discussion at a party. A friend, Jack, was retrospectively discussing the Watergate debacle. He suggested that one of the so-called "plumber's group" was really smart. I was surprised and somewhat offended, being self-righteous about that whole affair. I responded, "He was not too smart; he ended up in jail." I made Jack wrong, and we became involved in a futile argument, each calling on our resources to be right or to win the argument. My attempted "make wrong" could have become a barrier in our friendship; however, we both let the incident pass.

The ego is highly resistant to change and often refuses to accept other points of view. This is particularly true for us given that our ego-mind and ego-voice insist on righteousness about our interpretations. Our ego's reactive communication system is a self-protective, self-confirming cycle out of which no escape seems possible.

Our ego's perceptions are not true perceptions, but are based instead on evaluation and projection. Recall our earlier discussion about cause and effect in Chapter I. For example, "Joe made me angry" is the ego's perception (albeit an incorrect perception). You created the anger and projected your anger to Joe (a correct perception). It is your anger and not Joe's. The ego is very clever and avoids responsibility for its own actions. In this case, you create anger, and you project it to (blame it on) another. Then you dissociate from the cause, which you falsely perceive to be Joe. You appear to be the innocent victim, and Joe appears to be the guilty party.

The ego always projects false cause. Our problems appear to be caused by others. Then we become self-righteous to justify our blaming them. In doing so, we use our judgments to justify our self-righteousness. Thus we become imprisoned by our own ego defense system.

Assumption Six: There is another reality.
The ego functions through a split mind that leads to split realities. We become a Jekyll and Hyde, so to speak. The ego splits the mind and places it in conflict with itself; it separates and reverses our perception of cause and effect. The ego sees reality in what is external to the mind. Therefore, the ego mind results in misperception.

The true-Self reflects a unified mind and functions harmoniously, because it sees reality arising from our thoughts and beliefs, our perception and experience, not the external world. Thus it sees that our reality arises from within the mind.

The ego was described as a false self that sees a false reality. Indeed there is a true-Self that sees your true reality. True-Self is your causal or creative conscious self. It is the witness state or objective observer of your life. True-Self creates true perception and communication. It is the Self that empowers you and sets you free. The experience of personal freedom comes only through a process of self-awareness and self-realization.

No one can persuade another to change. Each of
us guards a gate of change that can only be
unlocked from within. No one can open the gate
for another.

— Marilyn Ferguson

To discover and experience that you create your own reality and, therefore, create what is true for you, it is imperative that you give conscious attention to your communication. We will look at the process of communication in the next two chapters.

Chapter Two Insights
A Meeting With the Creator

1. Recall a time in your life when you were totally satisfied with yourself and describe how you perceived others and the world around you. Now recall a time when you felt frustrated that you could not achieve a goal or that you had failed at a task. Again, describe how you perceived others and the world around you.

2. Identify a strong belief you have changed in your lifetime.

3. Describe something you believed you could never do but later found out that you could.

4. Identify ways in which you have been programmed by what you have experienced or believed:
   a. Something about how you think (e.g., I think teachers should . . .)
   b. Something about your appearance (e.g., I look good in/ with . . .)
   c. Something about your behavior (e.g., I am shy, funny, ambitious . . .)

5. Discuss a reaction you had to a particular situation and how you justified it. Include the S-A-G-R pattern in your answer. For example:
   a. Someone challenged a belief or opinion that you valued.
   b. Someone pointed out a failure of yours, which led to blame or invalidation.
   c. Someone pointed out a success of yours, which acknowledged and validated you.

6. Describe a situation in which you tried to be right and win in your communication in a relationship. What were you willing to do to be right or to win?

CHAPTER THREE

You Make Up the Meaning

The Morning News

Imagine yourself on a morning commuter bus from your neighborhood into the city. You sit down beside a man and as you glance at him, he immediately pulls his newspaper up to his face and blocks you from his line of vision. What is your perception or your interpretation of the incident? You will no doubt recall from the first chapter that you must consider the facts of the case. You sat down beside a man and glanced at him; then he pulled his paper up to his face and blocked you from his line of vision. Those are the facts. Imagine yourself in that situation. What would your perception be?

It was clear to you that the man did not accidentally pull his paper up to his face as you glanced at him. He did it purposefully. I posed this situation at a workshop and received a number of responses. One person said, "Right or wrong, I would feel the man was rude." A second person guessed that the man probably did not want to share his seat. Another person said, "He was probably in a bad mood. I know I never like to be bugged early in the morning." Someone else ventured, "He was probably a very nice man who was just awfully shy." Finally, and somewhat impatiently, a man in the workshop closed the discussion with the comment, "Hey wait a minute! The guy just wanted to read the morning news, and you all are making up your own little personal realities about him. It's just like the 'elephant story' (see Chapter I). Each of you sees only your own interpretation."

Obviously none of us could argue with this conclusion. Each person had created her or his meaning or perception from the very same incident. Even so, there was a point we could all agree on. It was very clear that the man with the newspaper did not want to have a conversation. And we all got the message!

You Can't Not Communicate

So you see there is really nothing to decide. You can't **not** communicate, so why not learn to understand your communication and how to make it serve you more effectively. All of your behavior potentially is communication. Do you keep your word? Can you be counted on to keep your agreements? Are you responsible? Moreover, how you dress, when you eat, what you read, what you do, all carry messages. Even a recluse communicates with nature, with himself, and to others the message that he wants to be left alone. You can be sure that others will get your point. My point is that communication may occur regardless of what you do or don't do.

To communicate or not to communicate is not the question! The message that is sent (created) and expressed by symbols or words is not necessarily the message that is received (co-created or interpreted). Others will create meaning from what you don't say as well as from what you do say. They may also create conclusions from facial expressions, body posture, and other behaviors and conclude whether you are listening and are interested in what they are saying. The possibilities that you create in communication are numerous. And usually we believe or experience that our interpretation is true. In fact, what you create is true for you, yet it probably is not true for everyone else. Just realize that what someone else creates is true for her or him. For example, you may believe in flying saucers, but someone else may not. The possibilities for miscommunication are boundless. You may even find yourself in the paradoxical situation in which you can't communicate, but you can't **not** communicate.

Communication is your aliveness! The only persons who don't communicate are dead ones, and even they give you a message: "I'm no longer in communication!" In fact, you are a walking communications system, which is what your brain and nervous system are all about. We communicate by sight, touch, taste, smell, hearing, and through spoken and unspoken languages. Our senses receive stimuli or information, our nervous system processes these sensations, and our mind, without conscious effort, concludes what those stimuli mean.

Communication is the key to understanding. To know yourself and others, to understand relationships and the world around us, we must first understand our communication, for it is through communication that we give everything all the meaning that it has for us.

It's Not Just Words

We often perceive our life and world by symbols we assign to them rather than by our experience. We have such strong agreement that these symbols 'create the meaning,' that these symbols become our reality. We live our lives not knowing what is true. Education and position are symbols for success. Money and authority are symbols of power. Happiness is found in material things. We may believe so strongly in the symbols that we deny experience without them. Yet we know that none of the symbols guarantee the experience. The symbol is what we think is true; the experience is the reality. Nevertheless, we live by symbols, and we often substitute the symbols for reality. The ego is not concerned with survival of the self but with survival of the symbolic self.

Words are symbols. We have a word for everything we perceive. Scientists create words for worlds we can't perceive. They use words such as "quacks" and "quarks" and "quasars," for how else can we know reality? We use words to represent concepts (what we think is so), and we use concepts to explain reality, yet neither words nor concepts are reality. And once again, we may become confused and think the meaning is in the word rather than in our mind.

Words may facilitate the communication of our meaning and our experiences, but they also may confuse. The same word can be used to represent many different meanings. We commonly fail in our communication because we choose to interpret the same word differently. This frequently causes miscommunication. I recall a lengthy argument between two men. One insisted he was enlightened and the other disagreed.

Each used different meanings for the same word. Most arguments arise because we use the same words but interpret them differently.

Be certain to note that the meaning we assign to words is vital to our understanding. One of the greatest barriers in speaking and writing is the meaning of our words. We may assume that the meaning of a word is implicitly agreed upon and that we both understand words that look or sound familiar when, in fact, we disagree. One of the major barriers to education as well as communication is misunderstanding the symbols that we use. The mind goes blank or becomes confused with each misunderstood symbol. Even when we communicate by words with agreed upon meanings, people may reach different conclusions. For each of us the final pillar of authority is not the written word but actually our chosen interpretation of it.

Communication is clearly more than just words from a popular song, "Your lips tell me no! no! but there's yes! yes! in your eyes." The expressions, "I heard what you said, but did you mean it?" or "It's not what you said but how you said it," may leave us in doubt about the meanings perceived. We often, knowingly and unknowingly, express hidden messages. The stereotypes of body language, from icy glances to raised eyebrows, are familiar to all of us. Albert Mehabrian, in *Communication Without Words*, estimated interpersonal communication at 7% verbal, 38% vocal (sound of the voice), and 55% facial or visual imagery. According to Mehabrian, nonverbal communication expresses feelings, likes and dislikes, beliefs, and disbeliefs. In addition, nonverbal communication may confirm or contradict what we express verbally. Presumably our body language and behavior reflect our true meaning. Have we not always known this? Actions speak louder than words. Most people who have a hearing impairment can learn to read lips and facial clues very effectively. People who have visual impairments must rely, of course, on what they hear and feel. Messages are symbolized by words, but our behavior communicates our real meaning, our true intention. Behavior is communication; it is thought and word expressed in what we do. We teach (communicate) by example.

The book *Being There* (Kosinski) and the movie by the same name starring the late Peter Sellers, delightfully and compellingly demonstrates how we can create our own meaning through the interpretation of symbols. Sellers portrays Chancey, a naive, reclusive gardener, who by misinterpretation becomes identified as Chance Gardiner, a shrewd and taciturn strategist. People thus turned to him for advice. In a conversation with the President and a powerful and influential industrialist, Ben Rand, the President addresses Chance:

"And you, Mr. Gardiner? What do you think about the bad season on The Street?" Chance shrank. He felt that the roots of his thoughts had been suddenly yanked out of their wet earth and thrust, tangled, into an unfriendly air. He stared at the carpet. Finally he spoke: "In a garden," he said, "growth has its season. There are spring and summer, but there are also fall and winter, and then spring and summer again. As long as the roots are not severed, all is well and all will be well." He raised his eyes. Mr. Rand was looking at him, nodding. The President seemed quite pleased.

"I must admit, Mr. Gardiner," the President said, "that what you've just said is one of the most refreshing and optimistic statements I've heard in a very, very, long time" . . . The President hesitated for a moment and then turned to Rand. "We welcome the inevitable seasons of our economy." He smiled at Chance. "I envy Mr. Gardiner his good solid sense. This is just what we lack on Capitol Hill."

Is it any wonder that communication can become confused in relationships, organizations, politics, world affairs? Is it any wonder that our communication goes awry? Perhaps we should be amazed that we communicate as successfully as we do. The exchange of symbols – words – involves an illusion of communication. Obviously the meaning in communication is conveyed by behavior as well as words; we must look beyond symbols to the process of perception.

Perception **Is** *Communication*

Your perception is your chosen interpretation. You probably have heard the expression that people hear what they want to hear or see what they want to see. We might agree that there is some truth to that; however, my guess is that most people would not agree completely with such a statement. After all, we don't really want to see certain things in people or the world, even though we do. Let's face it, some people have certain looks or personality traits that you couldn't miss if you wanted to!

Perhaps we don't want some of our perceptions after we have made them. Nevertheless, it is a fact that we chose them. The problem may be that we didn't know we had a choice. Believe me, I can relate to that in my experience, and you probably can in yours. Since we usually perceive with little conscious effort or awareness, many of our perceptions just seem to happen. Sometimes we consciously select what we would perceive, and at other times we unconsciously react to what we perceive.

Let's return to our morning bus ride and reconsider our perceptions. If you reacted to the man with the newspaper, you may feel you didn't have a choice about your perception. You had the idea that he caused the incident as well as your perception and feelings. And since so much of our perception, our communication, is unconscious, we think it is simply happening to us. Conversely, if you did not react to the man but just observed him, you realize that you did have a choice in your perception of him. Also you may realize that on the bus ride you could have attended to matters other than the man's behavior. You could have glanced at the headline on his paper, looked out the window, any number of things. But you chose, with or without realizing it, to observe the man's behavior. Moreover, you chose to make a judgment about his behavior.

I recall discussing personal relationships with a group in which a woman said she was turned off by a man who always expressed phony affection. The group identified with that, and several persons offered advice ranging from ignoring the man to telling him she disliked his phoniness. The group never realized that the woman's perceptions might be incorrect. Instead they shared a reality by agreement, illustrating that communication with others is based upon our perceptions. We respond to what we perceive. Since our behavior is governed by our perception, we cannot behave appropriately unless we perceive correctly.

Unfortunately, the group did not consider the nature of human perception. The group may not agree that the man is phony, and even if they do, he could be very sincere. Their decision could be wrong. Imagine the miscommunication that would result when confronting this man about his so-called phoniness! Misperception leads to miscommunication. Notice also that the woman made a decision about this man presumably based on her perception of him, i.e., "He is a phony." She now has established her basis for communication with him, and she will always be able to prove her perceptions. But wait a minute! What if the guy we discussed really is a phony? What if the woman's perception of him is accurate? Everyone agrees! This point warrants further discussion. Have you ever acted phony in your life and maybe with a certain individual in particular? Does that make you a phony, or was this just a part of your behavior? People manifest a variety of behaviors. Sometimes we get insanely angry, insecure, or arrogant. People often behave negatively. You may even express negative behaviors yourself, but is that who you really are?

How many relationships are impaired or destroyed because we perceive and communicate bits and pieces about one another that we react to rather than choosing a perception of the whole person? How commonly do loving and devoted couples jeopardize or destroy their communication and relationship by perceiving only what they can't accept in their partner? *Communicate openly, honestly, and without judgment about what you can't accept, and you will grow in awareness.*

People must be held accountable for anti-social behavior, and usually we don't have to associate with certain people if we don't want to. Nevertheless, we rarely are aware of our own deep-seated motivations, so how can we accurately perceive those of others. Misperception involves an evaluation (i.e., a value judgment that may be incorrect).

Our perception determines our response. A threatening or fearful concept, or one conceived as highly desirable, completely upsets our mental balance and we do react! People may have very strong attractions to one another, and those reactions may become the basis for a relationship. And ironically, the same people may experience subsequent negative reactions to each other, which may become the justification for changing a relationship. The honeymoon is over when each partner reacts to what is threatening or undesirable in the other's behavior. What you focus on becomes your perception, and your perception is the basis for your communication. "But he didn't put the cap on the toothpaste," and obviously you have the proof in your perception. You have the facts, but the facts have only the meaning you give them. The facts may or may not be significant.

What we perceive, we think we know: that is the illusion of perception, but perception is always below the level of knowledge. Perception is limited to partial awareness and selective evaluation based on judgment. And we know from our experience that our judgment is sometimes correct and sometimes not. We make certain observations that we react to or choose to give our attention to. We interpret what these observations mean. We may check and double check the correspondence between our observations and judgments, but in final analysis, perception is our best guess about what we observe. Perception is a "guesstimate."

What we react to we think we know. We misperceive the cause of our reaction as being external to ourselves. The making of meaning can be illusive and is powerfully self-confirming because we use observations to make our judgments, and we use our judgments to guide our observations. Thus, we often are trapped in our analysis and cannot see a different or larger picture.

A new minister discussed with a group of elders of his church his fear that some members of the congregation had reacted negatively to his sermon. As he had feared, several members of the church fidgeted and appeared uncomfortable, and some even left during the sermon. He asked for advice about his dilemma. He felt he had an important message, but feared it might have been offensive to some. Several elders offered advice to him and suggested caution, accepting the young minister's perception as correct. The minister had feared such a reaction, and his observations and judgments confirmed his concept of what might happen. Then one of the elders, who had appeared to react negatively, commented that he and some others had drunk too much coffee, and some of them visited the restroom during the service. He hoped they weren't the cause of the minister's concern!

Decisions, Decisions

The meaning of our communication is made by a decision of our minds and is witnessed by our perceptions. Each of us is guided by our thoughts, which we express by words, and our words represent our ideas and concepts of reality. Our concepts guide our perceptions or our judgment of what we perceive. Yet, ultimately, the significance is not in the words, concepts, or even in what we perceive, but rather in the decisions we make about them. We can relate to the concept that people are phony and judge their behavior through our perceptions, but how we interpret their behavior is a decision we choose to make. Our decision is what we believe, and what we believe, we think we know, for it was our choice to believe it. We have found the proof in our minds' ideas validated by our perceptions! This is the process by which we arrive at an interpretation. We interpret what we perceive according to our own preconceived values and judge where each perception fits best. Without awareness of the process, we have created our own reality. *We see what we believe.*

Different people may witness the same event but give it very different meanings. Sometimes people create incredible interpretations. I remember a story about a man in an antique store who spotted the kind of grandfather clock he had wanted for years. He purchased it immediately. When the shopkeeper informed him that delivery was impossible that day, he was so determined to have it in his house that he strapped it on his back so that he could carry it home himself. As he lurched down the street, he bumped into a drunk and angrily said to the man, "Why don't you watch where you are going?!" To which the drunk replied, "Why don't you wear a wrist watch like every-one else." As you can see, it's just a matter of interpretation.

If you know something is true in your experience, you

don't have to evaluate and perceive the meaning of it. Knowledge is realized or recognized through experience, not through words and concepts. Love is a word that represents a concept, but knowledge of love lies in experience. Either way, the meaning is in our minds; thus, we must look to our inner communication to discover the source of meaning.

Silent Voices

Thoughts are not merely something the mind possesses; thoughts possess the mind. We seldom pay attention to our thought processes, yet it is through this inner communication and through communication with others that we create the reality and meaning of our lives. Words are thought packages.

Most of us go through our waking hours taking little notice of our thought processes: how the mind moves, what it fears, what it feels, how it talks to itself, what it brushes aside, what misperceptions are made.

Our ability to understand how we communicate, how we think or talk to ourselves, can only be explored by observing our own inner communication. To communicate with something or someone does not require that we talk to it or them. Perception does require, however, that we talk to ourselves, which gives meaning through judgments and decisions even though we may not consciously realize we do it. We may or may not be aware of the process, but typically our silent voice intervenes and instantly renders a comment or decision. "And what silent voice is that?" you may ask. The one that just said to you, "I don't hear any voice." "What silent voice is that?" Try thinking without having your silent voice lead your thoughts and your conversation. Can we communicate without talking to ourselves? (The yogis tell us that if we learn to silence our inner voice and our continuous flow of inner thoughts and thinking, and if we can learn to quiet our minds and to meditate, we will reach a level of knowing without thinking.) To answer a question, your silent voice probably will first discuss the question. Try it and see. A strange characteristic of our society is that we all know that everyone talks to themselves, but if you talk out loud people will probably stare and talk about you. Their silent voice may judge you as different, or more severely as eccentric, senile, or crazy. People may fear you and insist that you be locked up. So, we just talk to ourselves without speaking aloud, and we pretend we don't do it. We call it thinking instead.

All right, so you talk to yourself, and even if others don't hear you, they know you do it. By talking to yourself you decide whether information you receive is true or false, reasonable or unreasonable, acceptable or not, and even worth the listening. Focus your attention on your silent voice as you listen to a discussion, or observe your surroundings or other people, and notice judgments and decisions your silent voice gives you.

In Chapter II, I referred to this silent voice as our ego voice; consciously observe its operation. It has a comment or response for all occasions and is always figuring things out. You know that if it ran your life, you might not get up many mornings. The voice often says, "I don't want to," or "I know I am right." Our ego voices are judgmental and evaluative.

It is possible to experience a second silent voice, which

is different from our ego voice. You may not have noticed this second voice because it is less assertive and often contradicted or drowned out by the ego voice. You may not recognize it if your ego voice insists that you have no second voice. Don't give up yet. Remember the old maxim, "seek and ye shall find." I call this second voice our intuitive voice. The Chinese call it the heart mind, or "sinto." You may discover the intuitive voice most readily by silencing your ego voice. The intuitive voice is creative and profound; it is the voice that people seek through prayer or meditation. Your ego voice may decide that this intuitive voice is too mystical for you to accept. If so, the ego probably will prevail and, by your decision, you perceive only what you want to. Yet, is not your ego voice equally mystical and difficult to explain? The ego voice is very persistent.

If you quiet your ego voice, you can discover your intuitive voice. If you expect it to be, "Ahem, this is God; Can you spare a minute?" or "This is your guru speaking," you will have trouble identifying it. But if you quiet your ego voice and seek out your intuitive voice, you can experience it. I can only describe the intuitive voice from my own personal experience. To discover your intuitive voice, attend to a problem or a question you wish to resolve. The ego voice in discussing the issue will hide the truth by confusion or contradiction. It will try to resolve the problem in the same context in which the problem was created. The answer of your intuitive voice, however, will transcend the context of the issue and reveal the truth. It will be a realization based upon inherent knowledge; actually it will be the correction of a misperception by your ego.

How do you tell the difference then between your ego

voice and your intuitive voice? Your ego voice is almost a perpetual companion that asks questions and poses solutions, but it will usually keep you stuck in a problem – figuring it out, blaming others, and looking for alternatives. The intuitive voice is selectively available to you, but it will not persist. Invariably your intuitive voice will tell you the truth, and if you heed it, the problem will disappear. The truth will make you free, but you may not like the answer.

As an example, Valerie, my wife, started working in an organization that was very demanding of its volunteers. I appreciated the organization's value, yet I resented that her service interfered with some of our personal plans. Moreover, she occasionally made trips by herself and might return late at night. I became worried and upset about her activities. We quarreled about it, and I insisted that she stop this work. I was upset about the matter while shaving one morning. My ego voice said that Valerie was wrong and I was right, that she was inconsiderate, even irresponsible, and that I would have to do something drastic. Yet, in a moment of silence and out of my dilemma, my intuitive voice said, "You cannot control another person." I didn't like what I heard, and my ego voice reacted predictably. But I knew it was true. Although I was very fearful, I immediately told my wife, "Look, if I try to control you, we are both imprisoned. I realize that I thought I had to control you for my own happiness and security, but I now see that no one can control another. But for heaven's sake, be careful." End of problem – beginning of a new experience in our communication and our relationship.

I recall another incident in which I, as a department head

at a university, was upset with a colleague whom I felt had been obstructive in our department. I wrote a proposal to our faculty to which he immediately sent back a very negative response. I was upset about his memo while I was driving to work the next day. My ego voice was running a very critical evaluation and a fault-finding analysis of my colleague. I was upset and did not know what to do about it. Yet, in a silent interval my intuitive voice said, "everything is an opportunity." Mildly stunned at this observation, I felt compelled to re-evaluate the entire matter. I immediately realized that the hypothetical case that my colleague built to reject the proposal was an opportunity for me to discover potential critical interpretations I had not covered. I revised my proposal to account for unanticipated objections. I started our faculty meeting on the subject by sincerely thanking my potential adversary for the critical review he submitted. And to the surprise of both of us, he advocated rather than opposed the proposal.

The response of the intuitive voice does not persist, nor do the problems it addresses if you heed it. We all have the power of an intuitive voice, but few seek it out and acknowledge its message. Our ego voice probably rejects the intuitive voice from fear, insecurity, or disbelief. Nevertheless, I believe we all have the experience of this intuitive voice in our communication. I call this a breakthrough in communication because whenever I discover truth – and the intuitive voice is always truth – then my communication is expanded. Once I experience such a breakthrough, my communication never returns to its original limitations in a similar situation. My future communication emerges as a new and expanding experience – a new reality.

The intuitive voice has been described throughout the history of science, psychology, and philosophy, and it commonly has been reported as the basis for remarkable discoveries. Intuition was the basis for invention of the calculus in mathematics by Newton and for development of the theory of relativity in physics by Einstein. Robert Louis Stevenson attributed his creation of the dual personality of Dr. Jekyll/Mr. Hyde to his intuition about the conflict in behavior within human beings (Jung).

And how do you decide in favor of your ego voice or your intuitive voice? In my experience the ego and intuitive voices rely on images or thoughts in the language we normally use. Yet another intervening voice must exist that I call the conscious or causal voice. It may appear in thought or simply as an experience of conscious awareness. It is a state of awareness or consciousness, a realization in which you know you have a choice! Although you are free to choose, choose you must, one meaning or the other: ego's misperception or true perception. It's up to you. In the next chapter, we will examine how we exercise this choice.

Chapter Three Insights
You Make Up the Meaning

We give everything the meaning that it has for us through our inner communication and our communication with others. Give an example to validate or explain each of the following statements:

a. I determine the meaning of everything I perceive.

b. I generally make perception (interpretations) unconsciously.

c. My perception determines my behavior and thus my communication.

d. I can change my perception; therefore, I can change my communication and my "reality" any time I choose.

e. The ego mind leads to separation and miscommunication; the intuitive mind leads to true communication and joining.

CHAPTER FOUR

Choose What You Want

The mind left to itself will spiral you downwards.
— James Clavell

Whether To Wake Up!

How many times have you awakened in the morning and found yourself in a dilemma about whether to get up? You realize that you don't want to spend your life in bed, but the ego voice is so appealing; staying in bed is warm and cozy, and it wouldn't hurt to steal just another 15 minutes. So there you lie in bed, apparently at rest, but actually in anxiety and guilt. Will you get to work or to your appointment on time? And for many, getting out of bed is only half the battle. Now you must make a decision about what to wear!

Traveling to your destination, you must compensate for time lost on your previous monumental decisions, so you are dashing in and out of traffic to keep your morning schedule. Your ego voice is scolding you when it is not attacking other drivers. Who wouldn't be upset in this stressful world of clocks and automobiles? And somehow without your awareness, your ego voice recalls a problem of the past, and your mind becomes embroiled in it. You become angry and upset, and you seem unable to escape the cycle of the ego voice and the feelings it elicits. Finally, you arrive at your destination only to search for a parking place. You find yourself wondering, "Is life really worth it?" You ask yourself, "How did I get into this mess?" And your intuitive voice responds, "What you choose is what you get!" You are startled by this response and for an instant you truly wake up. You probably did not realize that you had been hypnotized again by your ego voice. And what you face is simply part of the fundamental dilemma of the civilized world: whether to wake up!

Which Voice To Listen To

Your acknowledgment determines your reality. How do we learn to break the ego's spell and choose another reality? The answer lies in acknowledgment, which is your power of creation and the power of choice. The power of choice requires awareness. This may sound like double talk, so let's examine what I mean. You become aware of what you acknowledge. If you acknowledge the ego voice, you will be aware of its effect, but unaware that you chose it. If you acknowledge your intuitive voice, which usually is a very simple realization, you will be aware of its effects. Thus you have the awareness of ego or the awareness of intuition, but usually not the awareness that you made a choice. Your choice is exercised by which voice you acknowledge, for *what you acknowledge becomes your reality.* If you choose or acknowledge without awareness, you will misperceive that you are effect. To be the cause of your experience, you must choose between ego awareness or intuitive awareness; thus, true-Self is being aware of being aware. True-Self observes, perceives and acknowledges, and consciously chooses its reality. You must become aware of your inner communication to gain this double awareness. If you acknowledge the ego's persistent monologue, you have chosen the ego's reaction. Now you misperceive that your experience is happening to you and that you are the helpless effect. This is exactly how we are hypnotized by our ego voice. You may know that you cannot be hypnotized without your approval. Your ego voice with your unconscious approval talks you into a trance. You become a stimulus-response machine as you follow the ego's commands. But you can choose to be a cause, or you can choose effect. We are often baffled by this process, so we must learn about it.

> *The ability to choose is an active power – and the sensation of having active power is both thrilling and threatening, because it makes us want to change those parts of our lives that are no longer appropriate.*   — Caroline Myss

The real question is how to tell the difference between the ego's thought form and illusions, and your real thoughts or intuition. I cannot give you a foolproof method, but the results you get are always clear. The ego's messages always reflect external causation (projection) and lead to doubt and fear, anger and guilt. Negative judgments are always of the ego and usually result in upsets. The intuitive voice reflects internal causation, and is always peaceful and supportive.

If you fail to recognize the ego voice, you will experience

its reactions! If you resist the ego voice, it will persist. Just notice and release it. You cannot perceive your intuitive voice when your attention is on your ego. Put your attention on what you want. Did you ever wake up in the middle of the night and find yourself re-experiencing an upset or unable to stop thinking about a particular problem? Sometimes it seems like you can make no other choice than to dwell on these things that are upsetting you. When this happens, reinterpret; change your perception! Make up a new story; after all, who made up the one that seems to be running you?

Acknowledgment is power, the power of perception and the basis for all listening and expression. We must study acknowledgment carefully and learn how to use it.

The Incredible Link: Acknowledgment

What you acknowledge, you get more of. In its simplest usage, *acknowledge* means to recognize something. This is the usage I imply when I say, "just notice something." For example, "I heard what you said" is an acknowledgment. More profoundly, *acknowledge* means to receive as a fact, to admit the validity of or to confirm something – to give it reality. By acknowledging a thought, message, or perception, with or without full awareness, you give it validity and reality. What you acknowledge may or may not be true, but if you accept and believe it, it is true for you.

Acknowledgment may take countless forms and often becomes a subtle link, but it is an illusive power. We acknowledge by eye contact and by facial expression and gesture as well as verbal communication. The power of acknowledgment is not in the form, but in its origination. Our thoughts and expressions arise from a split mind and so does our acknowledgment: ego or Self. While it is impossible to describe all of the forms of acknowledgment, it is easy to recognize its effects: a message was (1) received, (2) understood, (3) agreed with, (4) disagreed with, or (5) not acknowledged.

One can learn to use acknowledgment to produce incredible results. Acknowledgment can be used to control and complete a communication cycle (i.e., you can stop, continue, or suspend another's communication).

For example, if I say, "It looks like rain," you can complete and stop, challenge, or suspend my message merely by how you say, "Oh yeah." Also, the communication cannot be completed without acknowledgment. Notice what may happen if you ignore or do not acknowledge the communication at all. People may withdraw from communication or even throw a tantrum.

A woman told me that she spoke to a friend at a cocktail party, and her friend ignored her. She was so upset by the lack of acknowledgment that she vowed never to speak to her friend again. Notice how you feel if you greet someone or open a door for someone, and they ignore you. Imagine yourself at the top of a stairwell, and someone below yells to you, "What time is it?" You do not fully understand the question and yell back, "What did you say?" And a return voice, "What time is it?" You respond, "Two-thirty." You wait for the listener's acknowledgment, but none comes. Notice that the communication feels incomplete or suspended. You may even sense anger or frustration.

Is Anybody Listening?

Listening is not a lost art; it is an undiscovered one. Communication depends on our ability to listen. If you want to communicate with others, don't be interesting, be interested. The ego tries to be interesting and places attention on itself. Self is interested and places attention on what is being said. Listening is an active process because you must recreate what you perceive through your inner communication. The ego does not perceive but rather evaluates and judges and thus hears only its own message. The process we call listening seems obvious and simple, but do not be deceived.

As there is more to seeing than meets the eye, there is more to listening than meets the ear. Listening, by analogy, is like eating potato chips. For example, what does the term potato chip mean to you? It involves a taste, a smell, a feel, an appearance, and a characteristic crunching sound. Moreover, you get the sound and feel by reaching in the bag; you get the smell and taste by eating the chips. Your concept of potato chips is the integration of these sensory experiences with the more abstract ideas and information about where potato chips come from and how they are made. And in the final analysis, the meaning you give to potato chips obviously does not reside in the potato, but in the decision that you make about them.

What does the term 'listening' mean to you? Listening usually involves appearances as well as sounds and many inner feelings. Your experience of listening is the integration of these sensory experiences, with your memory, your beliefs, ideas, opinions, judgments and knowledge. In the final analysis, the meaning that you give to the multiple perceptions we call listening is not in the messages we receive, but in the decisions we make about them. Listening is not a simple matter, but a complex perception.

If we consciously create our perceptions, and if we do so with full awareness, then we are the cause of our listening and expression. If we unconsciously create our perception, we experience related effects and are not aware that we have caused them. The more unconscious the experience, the greater the effect: we become hypnotized. It is not the perceptions but the decisions that we make about them that become our hypnotic commands. We can release ourselves from these effects only by conscious recognition. Quiet your mind. Stop, look, and listen.

Ironically, we give the lion's share of our attention to expression – talking, making speeches – but the basis for communication is actually perception. All of our expression, verbal and behavioral, is based on our perceptions of our self and others and of the world around us. Communication is like viewing an iceberg; most of our attention is on the visible tip (our expression) and rarely on what lies below the surface (our perception – an inner process that determines what we express).

Swapping Perceptions

Listening is an inner expression, a process of interacting with or talking to our self. I call this monadic communication. Through perception, or inner communication, we create our reality, and through expression we share our reality with others. When two monadic beings choose to interact, they simply exchange perceptions: you tell me your perception, and I tell you mine. We call this two-way or dyadic communication. The incredible link called acknowledgment holds this process together. Only when one monad acknowledges another do we have dyadic communication (two interacting as one). The nature of acknowledgment determines one's experience of oneself and of the other in what we call a relationship. Thus, two-way communication is true or complete communication, but it cannot be accomplished without acknowledgment.

When the listener is not listening, there cannot be true communication. I have heard that the average couple only communicates 27 minutes a week. Did you ever try to tell a story at a cocktail party and discover you had no listeners? Indeed, acknowledgment is the difference!

Transact/React: Choose What You Want!

Let's look at how two-way communication works, or fails to work, so that we can appreciate the significance of acknowledgment. I will start with what we are quite familiar with, communication that doesn't work. It ends in misunderstanding, dissatisfaction, and incompletion. For example:

Process 1: Reaction
   a.   You said, "I feel sad."
   b.   The listener reacted, "You are always sad. I can't stand people who feel sorry for themselves."
   c.   You became upset, and you reacted.

What happened is that you expressed your feelings, but the listener reacted and did not understand them. The communication was disrupted and resulted in misunderstanding and negative feelings. When communication doesn't work, it has the potential to get very complicated. Both parties make up stories to justify their reaction and often seek out others to agree with their position. Now they have the proof and become righteous and unforgiving. Battle lines are drawn. "I can't communicate with you; you never understand my feelings." Let's look at a couple of situations that you probably can relate to:

> Mary insisted, "John, you always have to have the last word."
>
> John countered, "I do not and that is final."
>
> Mary responded sarcastically, "Did you hear what you just said?"
>
> John responded, "No matter who says the last word, you always get your way."

Can you see that John and Mary each believed his or her own statement? They could argue to doomsday, but in each one's reality, the other one always gets the last word. So they compete for it instead of trying to understand each other's communication.

> John: "Mary, the movie starts in fifteen minutes, and you're not ready yet!" (Ego voice: "She is always late.")
>
> Mary: "You know I hate to get to movies early." (Ego voice: "He is always bugging me.")
>
> John: "And you know I hate to get to movies late."
>
> Mary: "You make me so upset. I have not enjoyed a

movie since we've been married!"

John: "That's the only thing I have enjoyed since we've been married!"

Communication doesn't work if no one can see the truth, and no one is willing to be responsible. The truth, with nothing added, is that John was ready, Mary was not; the rest is judgment and evaluation.

Process 2: Transaction

You undoubtedly also experience communication that does work.

a.   You said, "I feel sad."

b.   The listener understood and acknowledged your feelings; "I know how you feel."

c.   And one way or another you expressed your acknowledgment in return.

Amazingly, when communication works, it can be just that simple. Notice that the listener didn't react to or resolve your sadness; she needed only to understand and acknowledge to complete the communication. That is all that is required to have communication work. "I understand what is so for you." And again, acknowledgment need not occur in words; it often occurs in body language, emotions, or other behavior. You do not have to agree or disagree to acknowledge, however. The nature of the acknowledgment determines the nature of the communication and the relationship. We need only to interact to understand another's reality. You may not see this now, but if parties who disagree were willing to interact rather than react, eventually they would come to an agreement through a higher level of understanding.

One of the oldest, yet least used and understood communication rules is that you must first understand what the speaker says. A principle of discussion dating back to at least the time of Aristotle, which is perhaps the cornerstone of Rogerian psychotherapy, states that:

> *Each person can speak up for himself only after he has first restated the ideas and feelings of the previous speaker accurately and to the speaker's satisfaction.*

— Carl Rogers

Recall from Chapter III that we rely heavily on words to communicate, yet we know that words often are, at best, a near miss for what we want to share, that they are merely symbols and that each person creates his own meaning for those words from past experiences. We are also aware that people often do not disclose their true feelings in what they say. To recreate one another's meanings and feelings, we must be willing to interact or transact.

As I mentioned earlier, there are two sources of acknowledgment that you can readily determine in communication: ego or true-Self. If someone communicates with you in anger and you respond in anger, you give their anger reality by your acknowledgment of it. Conversely, if you acknowledge the anger of another with calmness, you may influence the other person to reduce or release his or her anger.

Let's use my own experience, which I shared with you in

the introduction, as an example. My wife, Valerie, was suffering from a problem with her hip, and I was fearful and concerned about it. I angrily scolded her in my belief that she was causing the problem from improper exercise. In short, I communicated from ego. Valerie felt attacked and responded with anger. She acknowledged my ego from her ego, and we had a futile fight about the matter. However, we could have transformed this communication very simply. Let's repeat the scene: I am fearful and concerned and angrily attack. I communicate from ego. But Valerie realizes that it is my upset and not hers, and she acknowledges my communication in a loving way; "Paul, you are upset about my hip, and I know you are worried about me." She acknowledges me with understanding, and all the steam goes out of my anger. I respond, "Gee Honey, I am upset; let's talk about this matter" (have true communication). By skillful acknowledgment, you may be able to lift someone from an ego state of fear, anger, guilt, sadness, or depression.

True-Self uses acknowledgment constructively. But by unconscious and irresponsible acknowledgment, you may worsen the problem. Such is the acknowledgment of ego.

The acknowledgment given to a symbolic world has created a false reality and a value system that leaves us pursuing empty and illusory goals. If, for example, money and importance are your goals and the acknowledgment you seek, when do you have enough?

Recall that perception is our chosen creation. We can choose what we perceive in ourselves and others. If we choose to acknowledge only our perception of problems and what is wrong, we give problems reality. In this way, we may create or greatly influence the reality of others by our perception and expression. As parents, we may shape unconscious behaviors in our children, which profoundly affect their lives.

Many people have accepted suppressive or inhibiting judgments, ironically most often made by parents and friends, and as a result are shy or much worse. The parents who overacknowledge (react to) problem behavior in their children or criticize failure have influenced their child to manifest that problem. For example, your son uses the family car to take his friends out for pizza. He unconsciously loses the car keys during the evening and calls you at home for help. You are already in bed, become annoyed, and overreact to the situation. You tell your son that he is irresponsible, cannot be trusted with the simplest of matters, and can never use the car again. This mistake by your son is given reality by another mistake: your overreaction. Irresponsibility is being acknowledged by irresponsible behavior. If the son becomes the effect of the parent's ego attack, the son believes himself (and not merely the act of loosing the keys) to be irresponsible. If such criticism becomes a pattern of parental behavior, then the son's response may be set. In future mistakes, the son will feel guilty and verify his irresponsibility in himself. The son's perception of himself may well become, "I am an irresponsible person" (because my parents said so).

If your child gets a failing grade in school, and you imply, or the child assumes, that she must be stupid, the child will perceive other "failures" as proof of her own stupidity. When people view themselves as irresponsible or stupid, they start to act that way. People become what they believe they are and validate their beliefs by their perception of their own behavior.

> *The real problem lies not in the physical constraints imposed by the external world but in the constraints of our own mind.*
>
> — Peter Russell

We can make errors real, or we can use them constructively as lessons to be learned. You can acknowledge what people do well and support them, or you can attack others in the name of correction. But our first attack is on the self, for our judgment is our creation and we suffer its effects (ACIM). The ego is deceiving and believes its judgment is caused outside itself and projects it to a false cause. Thus, we think our judgment arises from another, but our judgment comes instead from each one of us.

Dyadic communication is very powerful as it determines the nature of all of our relationships. If we are a parent or a teacher, our interaction with a child probably will influence the child's communication and experience of himself or herself. If we continually correct the child's speech in a negative way, the child may withdraw and not talk. This is referred to clinically as delayed speech. There also are other causes for delayed speech. But, if we are responsive and interested, the child will have a positive experience, which probably will enhance self-expression.

So what gives our communication meaning and reality? Essentially, the way we acknowledge it. Acknowledgment may be used for good or for ill to support or manipulate the reality of others. You can control others who do not know 'who they are' by your acknowledgment. And others may control you by their acknowledgment if you don't know 'who you are.' It is imperative to discover Self or Self power, choice, and freedom. The more a person is aware of his or her true-Self, the less that person will be influenced by acknowledgment of others. The less a person is aware of his or her true-Self, the more he or she can be influenced by acknowledgment of others and the symbols of the world. Responsible communication requires that acknowledgment be used by each person to support others in their growth and discovery. Look at the effects of acknowledgment in your personal communication.

Know Thyself. — Socrates

Transactions

What we call listening is usually not listening, but the experience of our barriers to listening. If we are willing and able to look at our listening experience with a new sense of awareness, responsibility, and integrity, we may discover that what we have called *listening* for the most part has not been listening. Listening presumably implies that we receive and understand a message. To do so we must recreate the message exactly as it is (i.e., receive the speaker's message with nothing changed or added). Instead we often perceive our ego system's evaluations, judgments, and corrections, and we never really hear the message. We drift into our own exclusive inner communication. Each of us is the source of our listening experience. If you have listening problems, don't blame it on the speaker: look to the source. Notice your own evaluation, reactions, attitudes, expectations, and decisions, and then choose what you want and take responsibility for your choice. But what if the speaker is boring, disorganized, or uninteresting? Everyone agrees! Fine, then you get to be right! But you still didn't understand the message or the speaker; you only perceived your barrier. So you flunk the exam and the course, you lose the sale, or you lose the relationship. But you get to be right! I have often seen listeners block out or even walk out of a conversation because they disagree with a speaker. If we can't listen to another, we cannot expand our understanding.

All anyone wants is to be heard and understood. Notice what is between you and receiving and understanding the message and the speaker. Tune in, listen to key words, and get the speaker's feelings. You can learn very readily the speaker's feelings about any issue he discusses. Listen to how he discusses his friends or family members or other issues. The feelings are identified in the message. You can readily perceive any special meanings embedded in the message. For example, "I don't want to be a *doormat*." "My father was *very* stern." Key words may be cues. Similarly, how the message is said often reveals the undisclosed decisions and feelings of the speaker.

The ego is not silent because it is not listening; instead, it is busy preparing its own oration or defense. To recreate another person's reality, the listener must release her or his self-consciousness; and become totally absorbed in another, like an involvement in music, art, or poetry.

Prayer or meditation is listening. — David Wilkenson

I recall an incident at a workshop when I was left without a partner. Another person, also without a partner, caught my attention. Her opening comment to me was, "I always get embarrassed if I appear to be left out. I was so relieved to see you, and I knew the minute I saw you that you were a nice person." We experienced immediate rapport.

> *So without any intentional, fancy way of adjusting yourself, to express yourself freely as you are is the most important thing to make yourself happy and to make others happy.*
> — Zen Mind – Author unknown

Problems in Self-expression do not arise from how you organize or deliver a message. Styles and forms are the illusions of communication: the essence of communication is expressing who you are.

I have known many people who hide behind titles and credentials, smocks, uniforms and badges, intellectual or brash verbiage, shyness, positions of influence, five layers of makeup, a perpetual soap opera, or even witticism and humor. Who the hell is in there? Often we never find out. You are not your necktie, your physical appearance, or your personality. You are not your vocabulary, your money, title, or position. How you perceive yourself is what you express. You are not your acts or your ego's concepts. And finally, you are not your fear! These can be barriers that keep you from true-Self discovery and expression.

Say what is so for you and take responsibility for your own creation. You communicate exactly what is on your mind, so why try to disguise it? People will perceive your feelings. If you feel guilty, people will be aware of it; if you are in fear or confusion, you express it. If you try to sell something you really don't believe in, people will perceive your doubt. Those who are aware know how to listen and perceive beyond your words. You will see in your listener your expression of yourself. If you are fearful or angry, your listener will probably reflect it. If you express joy and love, that is what you experience. Your listener is your mirror in which you can discover yourself.

To gain insight into the process of communication and miscommunication, notice the communication of others when you are not involved. Let's look at some transactions. In his book, *Love Is Letting Go of Fear*, Dr. Gerald Jampolsky, a psychiatrist, presents a vignette, which demonstrates the power and poignancy of open and honest communication:

I was called at 2 a.m. one Sunday to see a patient on the locked psychiatric ward who had suddenly gone berserk. The patient, whom I had not seen before, had been admitted the previous afternoon with a diagnosis of acute schizophrenia. About ten minutes before I saw him, he had removed the wooden molding from around the door. I looked through the small window in the door and saw a man six feet four inches tall, weighing 280 pounds. He was running around the room nude, carrying this large piece of wood with nails sticking out and talking gibberish. I really didn't know what to do. There were two male nurses, both of whom seemed scarcely five feet tall, who said, 'We will be right behind you, Doc.' I didn't find that reassuring. As I continued to look through the window, I began to recognize how scared the patient was, and then it began to trickle into my consciousness how scared I was. All of a sudden it occurred to me that he and I have a common bond that might allow for unity – namely, that we were both scared. Not knowing what else to do, I yelled through the thick door, 'My name is Dr. Jampolsky, and I want to come and help you, but I'm scared. I'm scared that I might get hurt, and I can't help wondering if you aren't scared too. I'm scared that you might get hurt.' With this, he stopped his gibberish, turned around and said, 'You're goddamn right I'm scared.' I continued yelling to him, telling him how scared I was, and he was yelling back how scared he was. In a sense, we became therapists to each other. As we talked, our fear disappeared and our voices calmed down. He then allowed me to walk in alone, talk with him, and give him some oral medication and leave. This was a very powerful and important learning experience for me. At first I saw the patient as a potential enemy who was going to hurt me. (My past told me that anyone who seemed disturbed and had a club in his hand was dangerous.) I chose not to use the manipulative device of authority which would have only served the purpose of creating more fear and separation. When I found a common bond in our fearful attitudes and sincerely asked for his help, he joined me. We were then in a position of helping each other. When I saw this patient as my teacher rather than my enemy, he helped me recognize that perhaps we are all equally insane and that it is only the form of our insanity that is different.

— Jampolsky

In the book, *Getting Well Again* (Simonton, Simonton,

and Creighton), the authors provide excellent examples of transaction. Note in these examples how considerations arise, how they are acknowledged, and how the directness in response leads to completion.

A grown son is visiting his father who is dying in a hospital 300 miles from home.

Son: "Dad, is there anything I can do to help?"

Father: "Yes, if you would come and visit me more often that would help a whole lot. I feel so much better when you're here."

Son: "Dad, I'm pleased that my coming is important to you, and I'm glad you feel better when I'm here. I'd like to know how often you want me to come back. I want to visit you, but it causes some hardships on my family and I'm trying to balance those out."

Father: "Oh, I don't want to be too much trouble to you. You just go about your life and forget about me. I'm an old man and probably won't live much longer anyway."

At this point it would be easy for the son to get diverted from the central issue and either try to reassure his father that he is indeed loved, or get angry at this apparent effort to manipulate him and make him feel guilty. His getting involved in either issue would prevent resolution of the basic dilemma. The son should stay with the essential question:

Son (gently): "Dad, you asked if I would visit you, and

I'd really like to do that. But it would help me a lot if you could tell me how often you'd like me to come."

Father: "Oh, well, however often you can. You know how often you can."

The conversation could end here with neither person feeling satisfied. Instead, it is important for the son to go back to the central issue.

Son (firmly, but gently): "Dad, how often do you want me to come and visit? It's important that I know. It does take some effort to get out here to visit you, so I want to feel good about any commitment I make. It would really help me if you would tell me how often you want me to visit."

Father: "Well, I'd like to see you every chance you get. I'd like to see you every weekend. I know you're awfully busy, and maybe just once a month...I'm not sure...I guess if you'd come to see me once a month that would be better than nothing."

Son: "It is a long trip, so I don't think I can comfortably make it every weekend. But I would like to see you more than once a month. Why don't we plan on every other weekend? I think that's reasonable while you're as sick as you are. We can check again in a month...I expect you'll be much better by then. But for the next month I'll be here every other weekend."

Father: "Well, OK. But I don't want to be a burden on

you. I hate being sick and putting you out."

Again, the conversation could end here, though it would still leave things a bit unresolved. But it is clear now that some of the father's fretfulness and self-pity comes from his difficulty in accepting his weakness and poor health. Still, he continues to need some reassurance that he is loved. The best reply for the son might be:

Son: "Dad, I'm sure it's tough being sick like this, but I just want you to know that I love you and want to be with you. It's very important for me and my family to be around you during this illness. It may be an inconvenience, but that's what families are for. I just want you to know that I love you and want you to get well."

The conversation ends with both people feeling good with no loose ends of guilt or misunderstanding.

As best you can, try to avoid phrases that deny or reject the person's feelings, such as "Don't be silly! You're not going to die," or "You've just got to stop thinking like that," or "You've got to stop feeling sorry for yourself." Remember that you do not have to do anything about the person's feelings except listen to them. You do not need to understand them or to change them. If you try to change them, you'll only make your loved one feel worse because you'll communicate the idea that his or her present feelings are unacceptable. Also, notice that if your communication is not acknowledged, if your questions are not answered, you must press for completion. If others do not acknowledge you, take a look at your own expression.

These excellent examples could be applied to all communication from consoling a loved one, to engaging in politics, to salesmanship, to a simple exchange of ideas. The interaction can be seen in the following diagrams.

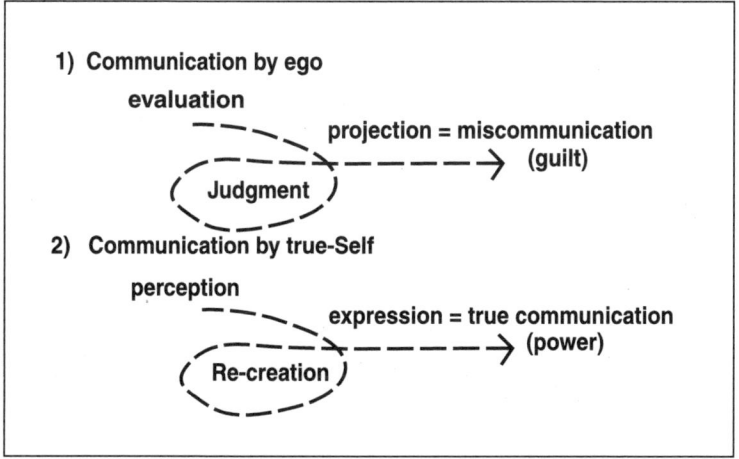

When you acknowledge the true-Self in others, you create true communication in which Self acknowledges Self. When you acknowledge the ego in others, you create miscommunication by ego reacting to ego. Self creates love and power; ego creates fear, anger, and guilt. What you acknowledge is what you get. Choose what you want.

When your communication is not flowing with acknowledgment and completion, you are experiencing your own barriers. In the next chapter we will identify the nature of our barriers and discover them as opportunities.

Chapter Four Insights
Choose What You Want

1. Record your observations for each listening situation below:
   a. I evaluated and made judgments about the speaker or what was said instead of listening.
   b. I observed a conflict between the speaker's words and apparent feelings.
   c. I reacted to the message and did not listen.

2. Give an example of an inner communication through which you discovered a personal reality that you had created.

3. Describe a situation in which you were confused about whether your inner communication was ego voice or intuitive voice. Describe the effects that would have resulted from following your inner communication.

4. Give an example of how your process of acknowledging of another person influenced your communication with that person and determined the outcome.

Problems Are Opportunities

Recognizing, Owning, And Releasing Your Barriers

All of your barriers are self-imposed. A number of years ago I was attending a meeting where people were sharing different impressions of what they had experienced from a presentation. As I listened with curiosity to what people said, I noticed that my ego voice evaluated and judged each speaker: "Wow, that person is inspiring. She is really bright." But the next one, "Oh no – what a bore. If this guy had a brain, he would have it out and be playing with it." "Let's see what the fat man has to say. He needs to lose fifty pounds. What a funny sounding voice." And this guy, "Boy he is a phony. It has something to do with his facial expression when he talks." Then, "What is this woman's problem? I don't believe a word she says." I continued to judge and comment to myself and to lapse into boredom until my intuitive voice startled me with an incredible comment:

You perceive only your own judgments.

People were sharing experiences that were meaningful for them, but I was not listening or understanding how they felt. I was just sitting there making judgments. I was astounded!

My boredom instantly lifted, and my mind returned to the communication in the room. People continued to share, and each time my ego voice started a new story – a judgment about each person. Yet now I perceived it differently. While my ego voice commented about each speaker, my intuitive voice told me to listen. "These people are telling what is true for them and how they really feel." For the first time in my life I actually listened. I abandoned my thoughts to hear what others had to say – I no longer regarded them as people whose looks I approved of or as people who sounded sincere or intelligent; instead, I saw and listened to each person in a completely new way.

I realized that never again would I experience people or their communication in the same way as I had before. I continue to make judgments from time to time, but now I always know I have a choice. If I am willing to understand, to recreate *the speaker's message, then "I can put myself in their shoes." I was deeply moved by this discovery about myself, and this discovery transformed my personal communication.*

The circumstances of my communication have not changed, but my experience is transformed. Until that experience, I had not consciously realized that my communication was blocked by self-imposed barriers. Most of my experience was based on my ego evaluations, and I had unconsciously projected my conclusions onto other people: "They sounded funny; they were phony; they were brilliant." It was all my ego system. Incredible!

Judgments are our ego's way of superimposing its own will and standards on others. That is, we frequently judge in order to categorize and to control other people. We do this to make ourselves special.

Your Barriers Are Your Communication Filters
Judgments

I made the assumption in Chapter II that each of us has our own unique communication system that is programmed by our mind's conscious and unconscious [1] records of all our experiences. Your program becomes your ego's system, the filter through which all your input in communication passes. To discover our barriers to communication, we must first look at our ego system. If we examine our own filters, we can discover why we accept, change, or reject the messages we receive.

Everything we perceive or accept must conform to our filters' characteristics. Signals or messages that do not conform will be modified or blocked. In this way, we filter our perceptions and responses to fit them into our judgments and beliefs. In other words, we modify or block the information or messages we receive to make them fit into our personal filters. We resist or block the input with which we disagree, and we modify or limit the input that we do not have the openness or capacity to accept. We operate like a resistance-capacitance (R-C) filter. [2] Again, your communication filter accepts messages with which it agrees, changes to its own understanding

---

[1] I use the term *unconscious* to mean any lack of awareness ranging from inattentiveness to complete unawareness.

[2] I use this as an anology with electronic resistance-capacitance filters because they are designed only to accept or to pass on limited or "filtered" information.

messages within its capacity to handle, and resists or rejects anything that does not conform, such as opposing beliefs or opinions. You alone can control what it will allow to pass, and you alone control the on-off switch for your filter.

In examining your communication filters, you will discover your own resistance to incoming information and messages: your reactions, judgments, and evaluations. Now look at your capacitance; that's your capacity to accept incoming information and messages. Our resistance to new ideas and experiences is amazing. Yet we all have the opportunity to open our filters to that which challenges our acceptance or understanding and to transform our experience of life. Each of us has the capacity to become the cause of our experience and to choose our own reality. Instead, we usually submit to our ego's resistance in its many forms.

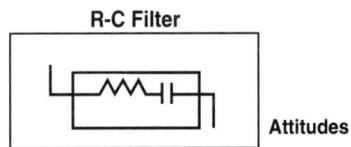

R-C Filter

Attitudes

Attitudes

Our attitudes and belief patterns, whether positive or negative, are all extensions of how we define, use, or do not use power. Not one of us is free from power issues.

— Caroline Myss

Our attitudes are determined by expectations, desires,

values, feelings, and past experiences. We have an unconscious agenda for everything: sporting events, plays or movies, and workshops or college courses. If any situation fails to meet our expectations or desires (or if we fail to have a good experience of ourselves), we consider it boring, stupid, disorganized, etc. We feel disappointed, upset, and even perceive attack if we are disappointed.

This is especially true in our relationships. We have very set attitudes and expectations in our relationships. We have our strongest expectations for parents, spouses, and children, for those whom we are most dependent on. Each relationship has built-in concepts and controls. We shall discuss this later in the chapter on relationships.

We have also developed defensive attitudes. In fact, our ego can be seen as a defense. The ego perceives attack and counterattacks even in trivial situations. Recall that the ego is on "automatic pilot," which constantly defends its image. Our ego voice expresses it in recognizable ways: "I don't want to," "no way," "I don't buy that," "do it yourself." Its message is, "protect yourself," which means, the ego defends its reactions. I know a man who took a job as a personnel manager. Unfortunately, he was unable to handle criticism. The first requisite of the job was to get along with people, but he was often in conflict. He was rude and severe with others. When he was asked to resign, he blamed his supervisor for not taking his side and defending him against his critics.

Another attitude is skepticism. We have relied greatly on skepticism in our society and civilization as an ego defense. In fact, people take pride in being skeptics and critics, yet often do so in a way which precludes their own creativity and expanded experience. This attitude of resistance and skepticism may be a manifestation of our fear of being conned, looking foolish, or being discovered. The ego is self-protective.

> *Our mind is literal. It cannot tell the difference*
> *between a perceived threat and a real one.*
> — Marilyn Ferguson

Concept

A rather homely woman joined me in conversation at a cocktail party one evening. She had a rather unusual nose, shaped somewhat like the beak of a bird; she had high cheekbones, and irregularly shaped teeth. She was tall and very slender, and yet, rather striking in her own uniqueness. She engaged me intently in conversation, and I was struck by her personal magnetism. We chatted at length and with great intimacy. I was truly moved by this woman, and my intuitive voice said, "She is a beautiful being." But wait a minute, this is the same woman my ego voice originally said was very homely, even strange looking. How do I rationalize this conflict? *Look to your experience. Truth is not in your ego-mind.*

Never judge a book by its cover or a person by their looks. My concept of a beautiful woman is based on the way that I have been programmed consciously and unconsciously by social criteria. By adopting these criteria, my ego system's filter processes what I see through this program, or concept. Indeed, all of our communication goes through a resistance-capacitance (R-C) filter I call concept. A concept is an idea or

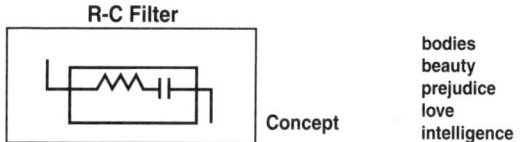

R-C Filter

Concept

bodies
beauty
prejudice
love
intelligence

mental image about how something should be. We can include in the term concept the images, ideas, and criteria we use to evaluate according to what we have been taught or that we choose to believe. This becomes the basis for a false reality.

At the level of experience or knowledge, however, we have potential for a different reality. Let's return to the homely woman whom I discovered to be beautiful. She did not meet my images or ideas of a beautiful woman if I accepted my concept as my reality. Yet, when I went beyond concept to the level of experience, I found her to be beautiful. If I had continued to filter my experience through my concepts, I would have missed the reality of the experience. Concept is an illusion, a false reality. Experience without interpretation, conscious or unconscious, is simply what's so. Notice how much of your communication and your life is based on filtering your experiences through your concepts. You can decide through your concepts or experience what is true for you. We are so programmed that our ego-mind interprets and invalidates our experiences in favor of its concepts and beliefs. People use concepts, beliefs and fear to filter out unwanted ideas and experience rather than to expand their horizons through discovery and creativity. Our beliefs, reinforced by fear, imprison us and preclude us from expanding our experience of life.

We often create a false reality by agreement to justify our concepts. This is an additional mental trap and an extension of our concepts, which permit us to validate or invalidate what we believe and think we know. Although agreement has only a face validity that we give it by saying, "Yep, that's the way it is," we can sure get upset if someone has the audacity to disagree. True-Self uses agreement as a working principle, a means for cooperation. Ego uses agreement as a concept to justify suppression, censorship, or control.

The history of science shows that agreement may have little to do with truth. You may recall that at one time there was very strong agreement that the world was flat. Moreover, that concept was reinforced by fear that if you checked it out, you might fall over the edge. Similarly, until the time of Copernicus, people agreed that the sun rotated around the earth. That concept was strengthened by fear of going to hell if you dared to believe otherwise. Advances in science and society often are restrained by fear of censorship and invalidation by our peers. Early in this century, physicists believed the atom was the smallest inseparable particle. Yet through the experiments of Max Planck and Albert Einstein, quantum physics was born, and through their work we now know there is no such thing as an inseparable particle. Experimentation has shown that the atom can be split into over a hundred so-called elementary particles, including a "particle" of pure energy, the photon (a "particle" of light). This is a new reality – a transformation in physics.

Acts And Pretenses

You don't have to rehearse to be yourself.
— Stewart Emery

All of us have numerous pretenses and acts that we substitute for who we really are or how we feel. We call this our persona. We then behave as if these pretenses were true. If you have your acts, they can be delightful. If your acts have you, you may never discover who you are. While we are aware of many of our acts because they are superficial and obvious, there are many that we are quite unaware of. We can liken ourselves to layers of an onion. If we keep peeling off layers, we can discover who we are as well as our natural source of power.

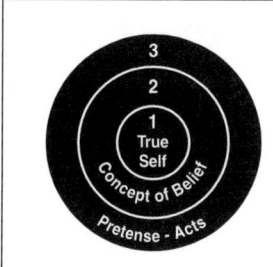

1. **You**

2. **Who you are afraid you really are**

3. **Who you pretend you are through your communication to disguise who you are afraid you are**

Acts and Pretenses

Acts are so well known to us that our society even stereotypes them: "cool cat," "foxy lady," "victims," "martyrs." There are lots of common pretenses: "I am a nice girl or guy." "I am a good boy or girl." "I am just a country boy." "He is a know-it-all." "I never tell a lie." "She is a sophisticated lady." "I am an intellectual." Do any of these sound familiar? Identify some of your own pretenses and acts. Your acts determine much of your self-expression; thus looking at your communication reveals your acts. Often everyone can see your acts except you.

If we were absolutely okay with ourselves the way we are, we would not need any acts. If we don't like the way we are, then we decide how we would like to be, and we pretend we are that way. That is true if you have your acts, your persona. For example, Mary is the original chameleon. When she talks to admired friends on the phone, she imitates the way they talk, wishing she talked that way. John can tell who she is talking to on the phone just by listening to her.

If our acts have us, we may or may not discover that we adopted an act apparently imposed on us. For example, your parents always said you were shy, or maybe you decided to be shy as a result of fear. The problem is that you forgot you made the decision. You did it unconsciously, so you believe you really are shy! Acts and pretenses vary in manifestation and origin and may reflect conditioning, fear, or guilt. Regardless, the process is the same, as shown below:

(1) You: true-Self.
(2) Belief or concept: who you are afraid you are.
(3) Pretense – acts: who you pretend you are to disguise who you are afraid you are or are not.

Peeling off the outer layers can be a remarkable and moving self-discovery that can miraculously contribute to your personal transformation. Imagine living your life out of shyness and then discovering that it is only an act. Uncovering this could lead you to discovering how you created the act and how it was manifested in your behavior. We will find the evidence in our behavior to verify whatever belief we have about ourselves because we express that belief in our experience. In other words, if you believe you are shy, unworthy, whatever, that is what your experience of yourself will be. Your act becomes your reality because you create it.

I recently discovered a deeply entrenched and unconscious act of my own. For as long as I can remember, I operated in certain situations out of what I call my unworthy act. Now that I am conscious of it, I can choose how to deal with it. I experienced it essentially as embarrassment, withdrawal, not imposing upon others, or an undeserving act. For example, many years ago I received an award for the most outstanding research article published in a national journal. I was so humble and unworthy in my acceptance that some people doubted my credibility. It may even be the basis for a "know-it-all" act in other situations. Conversely, in another situation someone challenged my research findings, and I went to great lengths to justify my findings. Yet later I discovered an error I had made. My discovery of these acts was an opportunity for self-discovery and freedom from an unconscious source of self-imposed suppression or need to be right and win.

In a lighter vein, I have a friend who has a sophisticated act. He enjoys listening to Bach and abhors Tchaikovsky. His palate puckers only with the best gin in his martini. He likes only Cuban cigars, and he is offended if he sniffs less "exquisite" smoke. He belittles lesser creatures who resonate to lesser quality music or cigars.

All of us unconsciously adopt personality traits of parents, teachers, and others. People commonly live much of their lives playing a role of how they want to be or how they want others to see them. The real person may never appear. You see instead Mr. Cool or Ms. Cool, who is always hip and sexy. Such acts can cost you the price of close, loving relationships. Acts come in all shapes and sizes, and only the owner knows what is under the pretense. You may or may not be conscious of your acts or of what holds them in place, but the program is there, and you can discover them by observing your feelings and behavior.

True-Self is your best act.   — Mary Jo Topf

Button Pushers

If you reacted before you knew what happened, you had your button pushed. Button pushers operate both at conscious and unconscious levels. They appear as emotionally charged thoughts and can be funny as well as hostile. Button pushers are automatic responses. It seems that you don't get to select them; however, you already did. Now you can only have what you chose. *What you choose is what you get; what you got is what you chose.*

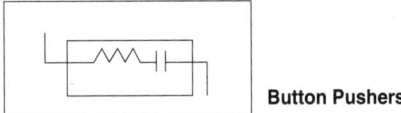

Button Pushers

You only know that you think or feel as you do, and you often don't know why, although I can guarantee you that your ego voice will instantly justify and explain exactly what caused it. Button pushers don't have to be good or bad. They can be of any variety of emotions and reactions. They merely reflect your ego stimulus-response, defense system. Whatever you create is what you get. Your thoughts or feelings are not in the other person even though your ego voice tells you the other person caused them. We cause our own experiences. You got your button pushed, perhaps by a pointed finger, eye contact, the sound of a voice, a TV advertisement, bad language, and often by someone's act. Take responsibility for your own reactions; it was your button that was activated.

Sometimes when Mary and John are chatting, Mary gets distracted by one of the thoughts that float by in her mind. She calls that "going south." When John is talking and Mary goes south, John really gets angry and says that Mary is never interested in what he has to say. John also acts self-righteous and tells Mary what an incredibly good listener he is. Mary has pushed John's button, but rather than take responsibility for his own feelings, John projects blame and guilt onto Mary. John believes Mary pushed his button, not that he made the choice.

Let's get a sense about how our barriers limit our potential and experience to expand our communication. The open square (A) in the following diagram represents your full communication potential. Notice how your barriers, represented in square (B), limit your communication potential. Indicate

A.	**B.**	**C.**
Full Communication Potential	Concepts / Attitudes / Judgments / Beliefs / Evaluation / Acts and Pretenses / Button Pushers / Communication Potential	

some concepts, attitudes, etc. that are a barrier in your personal communication in square (C).

How To Handle Your Barriers

Just as hostages sometimes become fond of their abductors, we become fond of the factors that imprison us: attitudes, concepts, acts, button pushers: ego.

— Marilyn Ferguson

Let's look at the barriers that keep us imprisoned, that keep us from full self-expression and interaction with our fellow human beings. Can you also see, however, that you can use your barriers for self-discovery and personal freedom? We have the power to use our barriers as opportunities.

The solution to the problem is very simple! **Just notice your barriers** – there is nothing you have to do about them. When you are not conscious of them or deny them, you are the effect of them. But by conscious recognition of them, you gain power over them. By discovering your barriers and being conscious of them, you can become the cause of your behavior. You can consciously create judgments and attitudes that support yourself and others.

You are not your barriers. Barriers are our pathways to discover who we are and to transform ourselves. Choose your barriers and take responsibility for them; own them, but don't justify or explain them. Don't make up stories to feed or support them. Tell the truth about how you feel without blaming yourself or others, otherwise you will succumb to negative feelings or emotions. Emotions are important in transforming thought to action. We must learn to understand and use our emotions in supportive ways. The next chapter tells us how to accomplish this.

Chapter Five Insights
Problems Are Opportunities

1. When you go to a meeting or a movie, notice the judgments you make about others and the situation (e.g., how others look and behave or "good" or "bad" points about the movie). Give an example of such judgments below to show how your ego mind interprets your experiences to validate (e.g., the speaker was dull because ... or the movie was boring because ...) its concepts and beliefs.

   a. Indicate something you agreed with.
   b. Indicate something you disagreed with.
   c. How did you react in each case?

2. Think of a time that you had a desire or set an expectation for yourself and explain what happened when it was not realized. Did you blame someone else?

3. Describe a situation where you varied your behavior according to the person you were with (e.g., your friend, your boss, your parents). What would you risk if you did not use these acts or pretenses with specific people?

4. Search your communication behaviors and list all of your button pushers (e.g., I get angry if someone talks about my appearance, ideas, beliefs, etc.).

CHAPTER SIX

Emotions:
Do You Have Them or Do They Have You?

Getting In Touch With Your Emotions

Objectivity is telling the truth about how you feel and taking responsibility for it. Emotions pervade our lives. A starting point in dealing with them is to gain a greater awareness of your emotions – discover them as they arise and tell the truth about how you feel.

If you examine why we withhold communication, you will probably discover that the answer is fear: fear about what people will think, fear that you will be discovered or embarrassed, fear that you will look foolish and be ridiculed, fear that you will be rejected or invalidated, fear that to think and express yourself freely may be bad or evil, fear of punishment (guilt), and even fear of fear.

> *The only thing we have to fear is fear itself.*
> — Franklin D. Roosevelt

It takes courage to express yourself openly. Are you willing to do it? Are you willing to express who you are?

Sir Isaac Newton not only developed the laws of gravity and mechanics, but also invented the calculus, a powerful mathematical system used to determine velocity, acceleration, and the shape and area of geometric configurations. He delayed publishing or revealing this mathematical invention because he feared he would be ridiculed by those who did not understand. As he anticipated, when he did introduce the calculus, it was considered "summing nothingness." Yet the calculus has evolved universally as the most basic tool of geometric analysis and integration in mathematics.

Discovering our fear is not as obvious as it may seem, even though our fears often run us. Yet people often insist that they don't have any fears. Some people may be so afraid or so used to being afraid that they never discover that their fear keeps them from communicating. Because of their fear they may not even know what it is they want to communicate.

The most subtle discovery is the transformation of fear.
— Marilyn Ferguson

Look at the emotions that arise in your thoughts and communication. All negative reactions arise from fear! When we project our fear externally to other people or animals, to things or situations, fear becomes anger and hate. Anger and hate are intense manifestations of fear that run rampant when our ego's image is threatened, invalidated, or rejected. What we fear intensely, we hate. Jealousy is a fear that someone else is better, greater, more loved, or has something we don't have. Embarrassment is fear of being discovered, how we look, and what people think of us. Condemnation and guilt lead to fear – the fear of punishment – and to the projection of blame as an ego defense (see "Projection," Chapter I). Guilt and fear are the greatest blocks to self-empowerment and healing.

Guilt and fear appear to be inseparable partners. Guilt arises from perceived wrong doing and fear of retribution: "I am in trouble now!" Anger is a reaction to fear of a perceived threat to the ego and has been described as "an attempt to make another feel guilty" (ACIM). Perhaps this makes sense in your experience. Notice if you use anger and guilt to control, manipulate, or punish yourself and others. Notice that people attack when they feel threatened. Let's look at some other emotions.

Shyness and boredom are forms of self-consciousness, of concern with oneself, and a fear of being discovered or intruded upon. The world did not vote to determine you were shy or irresponsible. Perhaps your parents did. But in the final analysis, it was your decision. Now what?

It is proposed that our natural state of mind is love. Peace is a necessary condition for love, and happiness and joy are love's various expressions. The natural state of the universe is oneness and love. In our reality this does not appear to be so because we experience many negative emotions. In the absence of love we experience fear, which is the source of all negative emotions. If we experience rejection or invalidation (not being loved), the ego projects our fear as resentment, anger, and hate. We say that hate is the opposite of love, but love has no opposite (ACIM).

> *Almost all the pleasures and pains of life are*
> *deeply involved with emotions. Most human*
> *conduct is the result of emotional forces even*

though we are tempted to pose as pure intellectuals, and to explain on rational grounds all of our preferences. Most interpersonal conflicts result from emotional stresses (e.g., anger, jealousy, frustration) and most interpersonal encounters are achieved through some kind of emotional communication (e.g., empathy, tenderness, feelings of affection and attraction).

— John Powell

However, let us not be deceived. Our perceptions and emotions are not caused externally by other situations and other people. Perceptions and emotions arise from our inner thoughts and decisions.

The Manifestations Of Fear

Your emotions may reflect what you don't say as much as what you do say. I call this a **withhold**. Withholds occur in many situations: to avoid losing (an attempt to win), to avoid hurting another (so you spare yourself), to avoid discovery (so people don't find out what you really are like), to avoid risks (so you don't lose), to avoid asking (so you don't look foolish), and to avoid telling (so you can manipulate).

Withholding your expression looks like the easy way out because you don't have to say anything. You don't have to tell how you feel; you don't have to confront, intrude, or push through. You don't have to be embarrassed. In short, you don't learn and discover and fully express who you are. In truth, your withholds cost you the price of self-empowerment, love, and healing.

People are actually *immobilized* by their emotions. Some people apparently cannot express themselves or choose not to because of fear or anger. A withhold appears to be an unconscious reaction, yet *you* decide not to communicate. You simply experience the feeling that you can't express yourself.

Carol, a very capable student in business management, had almost completed her bachelor's degree. Since her freshman year, however, she failed to complete a required course in public speaking. Now in her last semester, she had to face this dreaded requirement. In fact, she had started the course once before but withdrew after she fainted just before she was supposed to give a speech.

For the third time in a row, John made an appointment to see his boss to ask for a raise in salary that he felt he deserved. And, for the third time in a row, he lost his nerve. At the last moment he could not utter a word. He was immobilized. When he finally regained his voice, he rambled on about something trivial. Now, not only had he lost confidence in himself, but also he imagined that his boss had lost confidence in him.

People are often hesitant asking certain questions, or they have something they want to tell you, but they are afraid to hurt your feelings. When this happens, people may deliver **hidden messages.** "Where have you been?" may really hide a true concern: "Why don't you spend more time at home?" or "I have the feeling you don't like to be with me." "I feel lonely." "I imagined you were with someone else, and I had an attack of jealousy." Usually one becomes aware of a hidden message or a hidden agenda in communication. The true agenda, that of feelings, questions, or opinions, is the hidden message and only the speaker knows the game plan.

We frequently use hidden or covert messages and often fail to express what we feel and mean. The truth requires that we disclose with full honesty and candor how we feel. You may be reluctant to reveal your vulnerability, yet it is the only way to understanding. The price you may pay for not doing so may be confusion, misunderstanding, and bad feelings.

I remember an experience of some friends. After completing high school, Alice told her parents that she wanted to leave home and get a job. Her parents were concerned because they wanted her to finish a training program she had started. Her father, trying to appear objective but hiding his real feelings, said, "OK, but you will be on your own financially." Alice's mother became angry that her daughter wanted to leave home at this time. The communication was confusing and threatening for all of them. Suddenly Alice burst into tears and said she was afraid that if she didn't go she would be trapped at home. Yet she was afraid to leave. Her father then admitted he really didn't care about the money but felt she was trying to avoid finishing her training program. Alice's honest revelation provided the opportunity for everyone to say how they really felt and to gain a mutual understanding.

At other times the game plan is obvious. Some other friends are concerned about their daughter's weight, and their daughter is also upset about it. They don't discuss it openly. Instead, her parents talk to her about nutrition, diet, and exercise, but the hidden agenda is the subject of her weight. This discussion often results in an upset, and both parties blurt out hidden feelings or opinions in a negative way.

Many forms of our communication reflect anger and hostility. Sometimes we withhold these feelings because it is socially acceptable to do so. However, tantrums and outbursts do occur and result in *dumping*. Dumping carries no responsibility. "You did it to me, you caused it all, and I hate you." Good or bad, dumping often reveals submerged feelings.

When upset, we often blame another person rather than assume responsibility for our own feelings. It then appears that we are the victim of what someone did to us. We make them wrong, so we get to be right. Others often do the same to us. If you withhold your feelings and opinions, they grow in emotional charge and usually are released in a burst of irresponsible expressions. If you are open and honest about your feelings and opinions, you can communicate them responsibly.

Allison, one of my students, told me that her roommate used but did not replenish their food supplies. As a result, Allison became more and more angry with her roommate but did not discuss the matter openly. Then one day she became enraged and accused her roommate of eating all the food in the refrigerator. Allison was quite chagrined when her roommate reminded her that, in fact, Allison was the one who ate the last of it.

Upsets and miscommunication usually result when no one is willing to accept responsibility. If you do not accept responsibility, then you make someone else responsible by blaming them. What we must recognize in such a situation is that no one actually believes he or she is responsible. Our ego-mind will always perceive evidence that the other person was wrong if there is any possible doubt or any possible opportunity.

Our emotions limit our ability to expand and experience our potential in communication, as in the following figure. The square (A) represents our full communication potential. Notice how emotions, represented in square (B), limit communication potential. List some of your own emotional limitations in square (C).

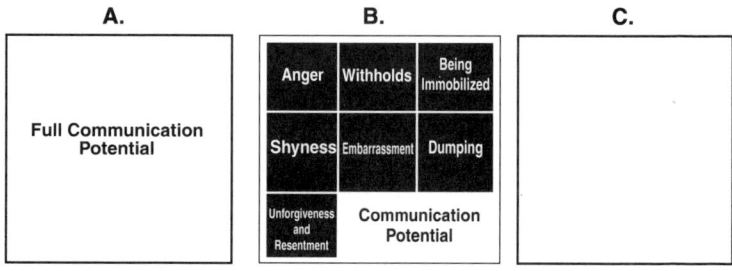

How To Handle Your Emotions

In dealing with your emotions, the key question becomes: Do you have your emotions or do they have you? Occasionally we experience it both ways. In other words, you may experience your emotions consciously (you have your emotions), and you may experience your emotions unconsciously (your emotions have you). Let's look at the steps involved in handling our emotions.

Step One: Acceptance You can start from nothing and look to your intuitive voice to create a new reality. The first step is to accept your emotions. Acceptance is a powerful place from which to start a process because it assumes no solutions. Ignore the advice you have been given all of your life, namely, that you've got to control (reject or deny) your emotions. Notice that if you resist your emotions, you hold them in place. What you resist, persists. As Oscar Wilde remarked, "The only way to get rid of a temptation is to yield to it."

Step Two: Experience When you are angry, be angry; when you are sad, be sad; when you are scared, be scared. We usually resist our negative emotions, yet we would not suppress our joy, humor, or happiness. The problem is that we process some emotions as good and some as bad! It is our social conditioning that becomes the problem and not the emotion. You have a right to your emotions, and they can be signposts for self-empowerment and healing. Experience your emotions merely by noticing how you actually *feel physically*, and they will disappear. When you try to control and resist them, deny or change them, you end up stuck with them. They persist consciously or unconsciously.

Step Three: Responsibility Own your emotions. They are yours; you alone created them. They don't belong to anyone else. Take full responsibility for them. *Don't project and dump them on others.*

Step Four: Appropriateness Don't act out your emotions. This is how problems arise. We have been taught to suppress our negative emotions because we may behave badly out of fear and anger, and what we do often is not socially or personally acceptable. Accept and experience your emotions, and they will disappear.

Imagine that a close friend breaks an agreement with you, and your feelings are hurt. You become very angry, you fly into a rage, and you blame and attack your friend. Although people commonly react in this way, it is not appropriate behavior, and they will feel guilty sooner or later in such overreactions.

Keep the situation in perspective. If people are not honest or are not responsible, and fail to keep their agreements, you may be ill-advised to depend on them, and you may choose to change the nature of your relationship with them. However, you may be inclined to attack in hurt or anger or to suppress your feelings and harbor grievances in such situations. All of this is an attack upon yourself.

You have another alternative. Realize that whatever anyone else does, you cause your own emotions. Just accept your emotions and experience them. It is okay to feel hurt and angry, but notice that to do so is your choice. Simply observe your emotions, whatever they are, but own your own thoughts and feelings. No matter what happens, we are both the cause and the effect of our thoughts and feelings. Notice how you think and feel.

I recall a time when I felt rejected. I then felt hurt and angry. I realized, however, that I had caused my own feelings. I then simply observed them, and my upset disappeared in a state of inner peace and gratitude.

Step Five: Integrity Tell the truth about your emotions. Don't justify them; don't blame yourself or others for them; don't feed them and make up stories about them. If you fuel your emotions, you will become the effect of them. A major hurdle is to tell the truth about your emotions, yet you can transcend that hurdle instantly by your willingness to speak honestly about them. The problem is to know the truth, and when you do, the truth will make you free. To start, look only at how you feel, for that is the truth for you. Lies occur when we try to figure out the cause, to blame others, or to justify our feelings.

Step Six: Choice   Choose what you get. Don't try to figure out your feelings. Some people laugh for joy, others cry for joy. We often do not know why we feel as we do, although our ego voice will instantly explain and justify our feelings. The secret of your power is choosing what you get and being responsible for your experience. And you don't have to like it. I'm mad and I hate to be mad; or, I'm mad and I love it. You created it. It's all yours. Choose it and move on. Don't look back; guilt is a trap.

Step Seven: Significance   Remember, you give everything all the meaning or significance that it has for you. If you want a solution, not an explanation, ask your intuitive mind – your true-Self – to see the situation differently, and your emotions will disappear. However, watch out for your ego. The ego is so persistent. Your ego voice justifies and explains your feelings. It will say you are angry because someone offended you or did this or that to you. We can easily be seduced because the justification looks like part of the emotion: "She made me angry." But the ego voice adds the justification so you don't have to be responsible. Because, because, because... when we project false cause, we say, "I can't communicate with you *because* you never listen; you are not interested in me; you are just like your mother, etc." Instead you can express your feelings responsibly: "I am talking to you, you are not listening, and I am angry." Or irresponsibly, "I can't speak in a group of people **because** I am too scared; I have always been afraid to speak in public; my mother was and her mother before her was and so is my great uncle." Again, be responsible. "I am scared to death to speak in public, and I'm going to do it anyhow" – or not. You don't have to. It's your choice. It is OK to feel the way you do. You are not a terrible person because you experience jealousy, anger, love, hate, joy, or fear. Everybody has experienced these feelings at one time or another. They are common human emotions, and you have a right to feel as you feel; you don't have to justify your feelings to yourself or anyone else.

Remember, you can't **not** communicate. People will sense how you feel so you might as well be honest.

> *Yet once we have dared to make our passage*
> *inside the heart (yield to our experience), we will*
> *find that we have entered into a world in which*
> *darkness leads to light, and there is no end to*
> *entrance. The fear of failure is transformed by the*
> *realization that we are engaged in continuous*
> *experiments and lessons. The fear of isolation is*
> *transformed by discovery of support. The fear of*

being fooled or looking foolish is transformed by
the recognition that not exploring is to be con-
stricted by fear and inertia.
— Gabriel Saul Heilig

Notice that your thoughts create your emotions. Since we have so many unconscious thoughts, we frequently only notice the feelings and forget that our thoughts created them. Select an experience of anger that you had recently. Recreate the experience and your anger. Notice the stories that you make up to justify and perpetuate your feelings. Now just experience your anger. Release your "becauses" and stories and sense how you feel – not what you thought – but how you feel physically. Let it be; let it pass. Now look at the same incident and create thoughts of fear about one aspect of it. Create a fearful consequence that might have happened from that same incident. For instance, you might have injured a loved one somehow. Create fear that you might have done that. Now release your thoughts and experience how you feel. Now let it be; let it pass. Keep repeating the incident until you experience a release. You may even discover something funny or happy about it. Now let it be. Realize that you create all of your emotions. They don't happen to you, nor are they caused by someone else. You create them through your thoughts.

What is to give light must endure burning.
— Viktor Frankl

Pretend that you want to ask your boss for a raise, but you are afraid you will be refused or rebuffed. So you decide not to ask for it. You are too nervous to ask; you get out of it... and you get out of getting a raise too. You are immobilized instead. You are saved from the ordeal; after all, you can't help it if you get nervous. Accept that you created the situation. Obviously, it is not your boss's nervousness; it is yours.

Now imagine that you must make a speech to a large audience. Create a lot of fear about it and feel immobilized. Let it be. Let it pass. Now imagine you have that fear again, and go to the podium and make the speech. Notice that you were frightened both times. The first time you yielded to your fear, and the second time you accepted your fear and spoke anyhow.

Transcending Your Emotions – Letting It Be

There may be times when you simply discover yourself in the midst of an emotional reaction. In that case, the preceding recommendations on how to handle your emotions will prove invaluable. Emotional reactions usually occur unconsciously when you are on automatic pilot. Nevertheless, consciously or unconsciously, you know you cause your own emotions. If you say you are angry, you are. If you say you are scared, you are. If there is a conscious instant in which you know you have a choice, release the negative emotions. Don't deny your emotions; however, don't buy into a negative emotional process if you can choose another way. Instead of anger, simply forgive yourself for having created a negative judgment.

We have been reared to believe that these negative emotions just happen to us. The only way out is to beat a pillow, kick the dog, or yell at the spouse or children. If you buy that belief system, you will act out your belief over and over again; your experiences will validate your beliefs, and it will become your reality. If you can, let it be, and forgive yourself for judging. If you can create a positive belief system and substitute forgiveness, why choose anger or sadness when you can create joy and love? Forgiveness leads to self-healing.

No one can be upset by a fact; it is always your interpretation that is upsetting (ACIM). I remember a period in my life when I was experiencing profound sadness. I tried to get to the bottom of it and figure out why I felt sad in order to overcome it. Finally, I realized that my efforts were futile. I simply released all efforts and even my interpretation of the cause. I was alone, yet free, with my sadness, and it was an exquisitely beautiful experience. In a moment of revelation, I was able to see the facts of the incident, which ironically had no effect on me personally. I could then clearly see that I was the cause of my own interpretation and also the effect. I realized that I need never be trapped by my own interpretation. I came to recognize the experience as self-healing.

Initially in this chapter I pointed out that emotions pervade all of our communication and experience of life. I stated also that love is the only natural emotion. Thus, it follows that love is the source of true communication. We must look more deeply and clarify misunderstandings we have about love and communication. That will be the purpose of the next chapter.

Chapter Six Insights
Emotions: Do You Have Them or Do They Have You?

1. Give an example of communication in which you hid what you truly thought and felt. What was the true agenda behind your spoken words?

2. Give an example for each situation where you used withholds in order to:

   a. Avoid hurting another (so you spare yourself).
   b. Avoid discovery (so people don't find out what you are really like).
   c. Avoid asking (so you don't look foolish).

3. Now use one of the situations you described above and explain how your withhold led to dumping.

4. Recall a situation that led to an intense emotion of anger, fear, guilt, or sadness. Use the seven steps indicated in the chapter to release your emotions.

CHAPTER SEVEN

Love and Power

Sources Of True Communication

Love/Not Love

Most of our communication is routine or perfunctory talk, just an exchange of information, symbols, or words: the social amenities, the news report, work or business talk, problems, cars, money, or politics. Often communication involves a disinterested talker "doing his trip" and a disinterested listener "doing her trip." Each one sees only his/her own point of view, and neither one cares what the other says or thinks. And what about our negative communication? Arguments, anger, and fights certainly are not loving.

There is another kind of communication, however, which is alive and vibrant and which involves yourself and others. Loving communication is happy, embracing, sometimes humorous, and joyful. This loving interaction empowers everyone.

We can thus arbitrarily establish a very simple dichotomy: the context for perfunctory and negative communication is "not love," and the context for alive, joyful, and empowering communication is "love." We can all probably relate to these two kinds or sources of communication in our every-day experience. I will discuss love and not-love later, but for now just recognize that the source is not in the words or even the subject under discussion. The source of your communication is where you are coming from: love or not-love.

It's not in the words. If you are confused with love as the source of "true" communication, the confusion may not only be in what you believe about communication, but also more fundamentally in your beliefs about love.

I am not implying that if your communication is not true communication that it is a lie; rather, I am saying that it simply does not come from love. You may need to change your definition of communication. Remember, communication relates to the experience joining – of oneness (being of one mind) – communion with another being.

A Second Look At The Source

To better comprehend communication that comes from love as opposed to communication that does not, let's re-examine the source of all communication. I made certain assumptions in Chapter II that our communication is a reflection of all of our thoughts, beliefs, and perceptions. I indicated also that we operate from a split process or split mind: ego or "false self," who you think you are, and "true Self," who you really are.

The source of ego is not-love or fear and uncertainty; the source of Self is love and certainty. This split underlies all communication. In other words, communication is processed by one or the other mutually exclusive system: an either-or system, love or not-love. For example, have you wondered how the same person is so beautiful sometimes and so ugly other times?

In Chapter II, I assigned certain attributes to the Self and other attributes to the ego. If you choose ego for your source of communication, you will experience and manifest only ego attributes: not-love.

Communication from ego is not sharing or extending yourself to others; it is self-centered, self-conscious, and withholds from or attacks others. Your ego-based communication does not give to others, but cautiously holds on to what your ego wants. Ego communication is not love; rather, it is false-love or the illusion of love: it seeks and possesses what your ego wants and desires.

The ego uses value judgments, condemnation, anger, and guilt to get its way. The ego is covert and manipulative of others for its own ends, for it sees itself as separate in principle: you **or** me! When our ego is threatened, we operate like a stimulus-response machine. There is no joy or power in ego "communication."

Unfortunately, people carry not-love (fearful) communication to extremes, and we see it manifested in anger, jealousy, and hate.

Fortunately, an alternative is available to us. If you choose true-Self for your source of communication, you experience and manifest only Self attributes: love and satisfaction and true communication. This communication is supportive; it works for you **and** me.

Our Confusion About Love: What Love Is And Isn't

The Ego's Projection

Given our ego's false concepts and beliefs about love, we have difficulty recognizing the truth about love, real love. We have created an illusion, a deception about love that has become so real for us that it is difficult to experience the real thing. We interpret many experiences of love from false beliefs and concepts about love, and our interpretation becomes our reality. Moreover, we are constantly bombarded with illusions of love (i.e., that our love comes from someone else), and we suffer the effects of this pretense in our relationships. Our misconceptions about love are reinforced by our falsely interpreted experiences.

We interpret our experiences of others by our concepts, judgments, and beliefs, and these may block or limit our experience of love. Each of us will impose our concept to make the experience fit. For example, if your concept of beauty is tall, dark, and handsome, or blond, blue eyes, and sinewy, then your ego-mind invalidates loving someone who doesn't fit that concept. If you believe you can only love your immediate family, then what you call love for others is fondness. It's not real love. You believe it is love only if another person affects you or if their loss or presence changes your apparent reality. Yet real love can only be extended to another; you can only have it by discovering it within your Self and by giving it away.

To expand our consciousness about love, let's clarify what it is not. Let's consider the false beliefs and concepts we commonly call love that arise from fear instead of love. The ego fears that we are not loved and confuses its fears, needs, and wants with love.

Miscommunication About Love

Sensual And Sexual Love   The ego projects its evaluations of sensuality to other things or people. Thus, through ego we see others to be potentially sensual if they conform to the ego's desires or imagination. The ego seeks sexual experiences then as though gratification were to be realized through that person. Obviously, feelings and experiences are generated by one's own self, and believe it or not, this includes sexual experiences.

Your ego-mind establishes its own criteria for what it wants largely as a result of considerable programming by pictures, movies, and social values and from your experience. Thus, your ego establishes its own desires, imagination, concepts, and beliefs, and it interprets your sensual and sexual experiences through them. In a similar manner, you select your foods, colors, clothes, and even your mate. You experience conflict if your choice is not consistent with your concepts or beliefs. Sooner or later (usually sooner), however, your ego voice reveals conflicts between your experience of love, sexuality, and relationships, and your concept of how your mate should look or act. Our divorce rates reveal that the conflicts often are more than people can handle or tolerate.

When the ego thinks that others appear to be what it desires, communication usually becomes covert to hide the real motives. Men and women frequently enter into communication from their ego's sexual desires, and desire becomes the hidden agenda. True communication thus may often be confounded or precluded between men and women. Hidden agendas lead to manipulation, guilt, and not-love. We often justify our sexual desires or participation by a pretense that "sex is love." In fact, "sex is sex" and "love is love," although love can be extended through sexual communication.

Sexual communication may or may not be an experience of love. It frequently is the expression of not-love, i.e., of fear. The ego-mind may project need, attachment, or illusory ownership to its sexual objects. We often justify our sexual motives as an innate physiological drive, yet these motives are frequently emotional drives based on insecurities, expectations, or unconscious programs.

Sexual communication as an extension of love results from the extension of true-Self and may be part of the celebration of love. Sensuality or sexuality, of course, are not inherently expressions of love. When either becomes an end unto itself, miscommunication likely results.

Acts And Pretenses If you love someone, you try to impress them. That's love! But is it really? No! That is trying to impress someone from fear that you are not OK the way you are. The ego-mind wishes to impress; it admonishes us to act nice, act polite—and whatever you do, you must keep up the act for fear of losing the love. The irony of acts is that you act one way, but your partner acts another. You "fall in love" with each other's acts (persona), and when the real people emerge, you both eventually have ego attacks and consequently some adjusting to do, a realignment or separation. Having to be or having to have someone else be a certain way is not love. It's called, "you can't make it with me the way you are: you no longer fit my pictures."

John is courting Mary, and he takes her to elegant restaurants in a luxurious car, buys her expensive gifts, etc. She is blown away with his magnificence. John impressed Mary with a big act. What happened? He expressed his "not OK the way he is-ness," and she expressed her impressionable-ness. But it was not love, just a pretense.

Need   A great love song of bygone days was called "I Need You," next line – "I can't live without you." Or what about, "It must be you or no one, or else I'm through with love." Now that is really, real love – wow! Or is it? No, that is called needing someone; "I'm not complete myself but I think you can pull me through." "I'll do anything I must to keep you." No choice, "I gotta' have you." This kind of emotion might be fun for a day or so, but you can't really love someone if you need them. And if someone needs you that badly, it could become stifling.

Two halves don't make a whole.

— Stewart Emery

Needing someone is a barrier, an experience of insecurity. This is probably where the expression "opposites attract" arose. You look to others to find what you lack in yourself. Opposites probably attract, but if you want that relationship to work, it will take some adjustment.

For example, one member of a couple is very outgoing, loves people, parties, and a good time. The other is introverted, likes privacy and solitude. Will one contract, will the other expand, or will they compromise to be unhappily comfortable with each other ever after?

Many people marry opposites out of need, and if each is supportive and committed, it can be a great opportunity for growth. But marriage rarely comes out that way. Stewart Emery points out that if neither person in a relationship senses their own completeness, then that incompleteness is a barrier to a full and loving relationship. If the relationship is built on need, then one person will cling to the other person. Two choices: cling to each other for mutual security, or support each other and grow. A relationship based on need may stifle opportunity for growth and freedom, for self-realization. "Need" is a trap for both members of a relationship.

It is not nice to be needed.
— Stewart Emery

Everyone requires personal growth and exploration. If your happiness or sense of completion is to control or be controlled, you have given up your power and your freedom. Your relationship is an entanglement. You must then manipulate and control the other person because he or she holds your happiness and security.

Manipulation If you loved me, you would _____ (fill in the blank). Covert communication arises out of fear and often is used to control and manipulate others. If you experience that your happiness depends on controlling your partner, you must really love them. Right? No! You just feel insecure and want to control them.

For example, John and Mary's children are adults now,

and Mary wants to return to college. John gets scared: "She may fall for her professor; she may get smart and leave me." Mary submits to John's fear, which he justifies with, "I want my meals on time. Who is going to clean the house?" Or he threatens: "Make a choice, home or college." Or hidden messages, "I think I will have a night or two out a week myself …." Love? No. This is just covert communication out of John's fear, and manipulation to subvert his fear.

Expectations, Pictures, And Fantasies Our pictures and beliefs about love are that love is scarce. If you find it, hang on to it. Oh boy, you found someone you love! (Who knows, it could even be the person you are married to or going with!) You've found the only one. But the ego does not know what it wants. Its evaluation never ceases, and soon it denies its own choice. The one you chose is not *the one*, so you must search again until you find another who obviously is *the one*. Save your love. Too bad you married your mistake. Now what can you do if the "right" one does appear? Your life is wasted on the wrong one. If only you had found the right one, you would have been enchanted for life.

The ego's fantasies never cease, but if we stop living in them, we could celebrate the relationship we already have.

Jealousy Jealousy is not-love. If we believe that our love, our well- being, and our ego's image of its survival depends on another person, then at some level we fear or hate as well as love that person. If we look to the other person for validation, happiness, security, and survival, we believe we must control that person. If they value another more than us, we must attack that person's image. The passion of jealousy may become "grounds" for murder if the threat is sufficiently great. That's how the ego's insanity plays out. But is this love? No. Jealousy is fear without limit, and we hate, destroy, and murder out of fear.

Protecting Others Have you ever noticed how much of our communication is about protecting others from hurt or harm? We frequently insist that we cannot tell others the truth (our perception of the truth) because we do not want to hurt their feelings. Why do we become a self-appointed protector of others? This feigned protection is not love. Whose feelings are we trying to spare? At least tell yourself the truth. The hidden agenda is not love; it is protecting one's own interests or feelings in the name of another.

Conditional Love "What have you done for me lately?" This question signals conditional love. Sometimes marriage is a series of negotiations.

"John, on our honeymoon you promised always to take the garbage out. You didn't tonight, so I don't love you anymore. I'm going home to mother." John counters, "Mary, I remember at our wedding, you promised never to gain another pound. You have gained 35 pounds since then, so I hope you do go home to your mother. If her cooking doesn't make you lose weight, nothing will."

Conditional love is a common form of miscommunication of love. Conditional love is self-centeredness and the hallmark of ego involvement. Your ego projects to your mate the way he or she should be to gratify your wishes. Your ego will always project some form of imperfection to others and particularly to one it holds as its own. After all, the world will appraise you based on the mate you chose.

From your ego's perspective, people must be a certain way to obtain its approval, and especially those that the ego identifies with most closely or projects its identity to. Conditional love requires that your expectations be met in order for others to have your approval.

What we commonly describe as love (or at least the symptoms of love) is not love at all. What love songs, magazines, movies, and TV shows typically portray as love is instead romance. Unfortunately many of our beliefs and concepts arise from these dramas of life that we consciously and unconsciously accept as valid expressions of love.

Love is not an act or need, nor is it jealousy, manipulation, or a conditional experience. These all are manifestations of fear. While love may be the cure, our concept of love is part of the illness. Perhaps we need to discover a new reality of love.

The Reality Of Love
Unconditional Love

> *This energy of unconditional love is the power*
> *behind creation.* — Wayne Dyer

The "true Self" experiences *itself* and all other *selves* as complete and whole within "its Self," and it experiences this inner wholeness or oneness as a state of unconditional love. Remarkably then, it follows that the absence of love, defined as fear, is non-existent in this state of unconditional love. In other words, the true-Self recognizes that love is its natural state.

We talk about love and our language addresses love as though all love is conditional (i.e., directed to a specific person or thing or object). For example, our most common expression of love is "I love you." However, unconditional love has no object, otherwise it would be conditional. Unconditional love is simply a state of oneness in which love is the only state and in which the true-Self is an extension of unconditional love. Consequently, the Self extends its oneness, or love, unconditionally to everyone and everything it looks upon. The more we extend our love – the more we give it away – the more we experience love and joy, and gratitude.

For example, let's say that Mary feels hurt and angry because John is often critical of her regarding a variety of things. She confronts John and tells him that he is too critical and that she is simply not going to tolerate it anymore.

John, in a rare moment, rises to the occasion. "Mary, I apologize. Please don't pay any attention to my thoughtless criticisms whatever they may be. The problem is that I often forget who I am, and when I do, I become fearful and upset, and I criticize others and overreact. But please know that my love for you comes from a very deep place within me. I can't begin to explain it, but my love for you does not really change despite our upsets with each other. If I criticize you, it is because I have forgotten who I am and has nothing to do with you. When I know who I am, I love you unconditionally. You are a beautiful and wonderful being just the way you are, and I know that you know that too. I will do my very best to treat you respectfully, and anytime I forget, please remind me."

Unconditional love is one. It has no separate parts and no degrees, no kinds, or levels, no divergences or distinctions. It is unchanged throughout. It never alters with a person or a circumstance. We think love can be withheld for some and be bestowed on others. Love cannot judge. Its meaning lies in oneness. Love is a law with no opposite.

— ACIM

Self-Love Self-love, unfortunately, has been confused with narcissism: being self-centered or enraptured with one's egocentric image. Yet narcissism is a deception of the ego.

The ego is never satisfied, for it doubts its own creations. Thus, narcissism is a deeply buried act, a pretense of self-love that hides the ego's own self-hatred. The reality of love, including self-love, does not depend on conditions and can only exist in the absence of the ego.

Recall a time when you were not OK with yourself, when you felt humiliated or unworthy. How did you feel about yourself and how did you feel about others? Can you love others when you do not love yourself? The only way to know and express love is to find love within, to experience yourself as whole and complete. This is true Self-love. You don't have to look for love when love is where you come from.

The Essence Of Love When we say we love someone or something, we actually experience our own essence and we call that essence of *ourself* the experience of *love*. *Being in love* is being aware that you cause your feelings, not the other person. You can extend your love to anyone and anything you choose.

In contrast, *falling in love* appears to be something that happens to you. Your experience then appears to be caused by the object of your love, and you are the effect. *Falling in love* is the state in which the ego projects false cause to a source outside you and becomes dependent on that source. Falling in love is an illusion. If that source doesn't respond, the ego experiences turmoil and rejection. *Being in love* is the state in which true-Self extends its love and knows that it is cause.

I know a woman who, although married for years, made a decision in the first several months of her marriage that she had made a mistake. The man she married was not *the one*. She feels her husband is not her equal in physical attractiveness, and her pride demands that she withhold her love. She has told many of her friends that she is saving her love for someone worthy. Several times she has fallen in love, but always with someone else's husband, and her love was never returned. She hasn't the faintest awareness that she is the author of her drama; instead, she sees herself as a hapless victim. And what about her husband? He travels a lot.

True Communication About Love

Beyond Barriers The ego's expressions of "love" (need, control and manipulation, jealousy) are barriers to our experience and expression of love. We mistake these barriers as the experience of love. We deny our true expression of love for others by our barriers, by our fears, our conscious and unconscious programs, and our beliefs, standards, and expectations.

For example, you can't love anyone who is unclean, improperly dressed, has a beard, is black, white, or yellow. All that separates you and love for others are your own personal barriers, which may be cloaked in the ego's arrogance, hostility, or indifference.

I am reminded of a scene from Erich Remarque's novel, *All Quiet on the Western Front*. A battle rages at night, which culminates in hand-to-hand combat in the trenches. A soldier kills his foe with his bayonet and falls exhausted and unconscious beside his vanquished enemy. At daylight he awakens beside the corpse. He compulsively stares at his fallen enemy. Eventually he begins to examine his enemy's features, his clothing, and his personal effects. He examines the dead man's wallet and discovers pictures of his wife and children. As he studies them, he is overcome with grief. He begins weeping and in remorse hugs and cradles the former enemy's corpse, weeping in his sorrow.

In one instant we may kill another from fear and threat to our survival. In the next instant, if the threat is removed, we may experience love and compassion for that same person. When the barriers are removed and we release our fear, grievances, or hostility, we experience a natural state of love. Love is all-encompassing. Love is the nature of our reality.

Empowering Communication *Love is Power. Power is Love. Love and Power are functions of communication.* Love is empowering yourself and others to reach their fullest potential, including latent potential. Love is self-empowerment and healing.

*Because love has such power, we come to know
this energy in stages.*

— Caroline Myss

The ego would misinterpret love to justify its own perceptions and to determine the goals for its *loved* ones. This is the ego's arrogance disguised by a noble purpose. The illusions of love expressed by the ego do not empower but instead weaken both giver and receiver. Love demands courage and commitment to support others to be, to grow, and to discover, and recognizes error and suffering as part of the empowering process. The ego's miscommunication seeks to control, invalidate, diminish, and weaken. True-Self and true communication releases, validates, and empowers.

The illusion of love as expressed by the ego would have us believe that love is limited to special ones and only when our conditions are met. Ego says that others control our love and power; true-Self is an expression of love. We will examine these premises in the following chapter and discover that relationships can be a source of fear or a source of love and healing.

Chapter Seven Insights
Love and Power

1. Describe some of your barriers to love (e.g., people must look a certain way, or I can only love certain people).

2. Describe a relationship in your life based on conditional love.

3. Think of an instance in your life where guilt and fear were used in the name of love.

4. Think of a close relationship that you have and indicate the characteristics that bond the relationship. List these characteristics and how they are conditional and externally dependent.

5. Describe a relationship in your life based on unconditional love.

CHAPTER EIGHT

Relationships: A Mirror of Yourself
Communication Is The Bridge

*No man is an island, entire of itself; every man
is a piece of the continent, a part of the main.*

— John Donne

Communication is the bridge between the island and the main; it expresses the relationship between you and others. Each relationship appears to be different not only because of ever-changing personalities, but because of ever-changing experiences of one's self. You create your experience of yourself, others, and your relationships through communication. You are empowered to make your relationships work, if you choose to do so. In each relationship, we have to ask ourselves: am I willing to make it work? You may have to give up your expectations that the relationship be the way you want it to be (e.g., will you let others have their own experience of the relationship or must it be your way?) Do you give special assignments to each relationship and evaluate it by whether others carry out your plan? If you accept others the way they are, you can have peace and love in your relationships. If you demand that others carry out your wishes against their own, you will experience entanglement.

Self-Discovery Through Relationships

Communication in relationships is a process of self-discovery. Relationships are mirrors in which we see different images of ourselves. Obviously, you experience different communication in different relationships. What may be less obvious is that each person with whom you communicate provides you with a different experience of yourself. Thus, you explore and experience who you are in every relationship, for what you experience is your projections of yourself in others.

> *I learn most about myself by observing myself*
> *in relation to others. When I examine myself by*
> *myself, I am usually examining the results of a*
> *previous encounter.*
>
> — Hugh Prather

Self-Concepts

Generally, we see ourselves and others through concepts, ideas, images, and beliefs rather than by experience. Instead of merely communicating out of our experience of relationships, we impose our concepts, filter our experience through the concepts, and create illusionary communication. For example, you meet someone who has an unkempt beard. Your concept (or belief) is that people who have such beards are not friendly. Consequently, you create and experience that such people are unfriendly, and in doing so create your experience to validate your concept. Now you have the proof. Granted, we talk about different subjects with different people and communicate differently with different people; however, that is not my point. The point is what you see (actually what you project) in other people is what you get.

> *No matter what we talk about we talk about ourselves.*
>
> — Wendell Johnson

You also communicate from a concept of yourself rather than your experience of yourself. For example, if I see myself as a professor, I may communicate in a way I think a professor should communicate. My concept of professor is doing the talking, not me. Now, everybody knows that professors use big words, act intellectually, and smoke a pipe. Some of my friends started to smoke a pipe as soon as they received a doctor's degree. Do you communicate from "who you are" or from your concept of yourself?

Self-Discovery

> *Nothing, including you, exists by itself. This is an illusion of words. You are a relationship ever changing.*
>
> — Hugh Prather

Another way to look at concept versus true-Self in communication is how we relate to certain people. You may, for example, communicate differently with your boss than with your spouse. You communicate differently not merely because of different subjects that you talk about, but also because you have different concepts of relationships. If you don't communicate from "who you are," regardless of the person with whom you are interacting, you are expressing a concept of yourself and others. If you are very careful about how you talk to your boss, it may be because you fear that relationship or because you defer who you are to a concept of authority. If you hide, defer, or exaggerate the real you, then you do not enjoy true Self-expression. Do you discover the same you in each relationship? Is it you being who you are, or is it you being how you think you have to be? Do you shrink and turn shy with your boss? Are you a shrew with your spouse yet sweet to little old ladies and children, or are you who you are in all your relationships? If you are not, try it. It can be an incredibly freeing experience.

Self-Disclosure

> *No human can come to know himself except*
> *as an outcome of disclosing himself to another*
> *person.*
> — Sidney M. Jourard

If we have nothing to hide, we can be open and free and invulnerable in our communication and relationships. Even more remarkably, we can push through our images and fears, our ego's creations, and discover our true-Self. We can empower ourselves and others through courage and integrity. The more we have to hide, the more guarded, defensive, and reactive we become, and the more vulnerable we are in our communication and relationships. However, be appropriate. We don't have to tell everything we know. For example, John and Mary dined at an elegant restaurant with some friends whom John wanted to impress. Out of the blue, Mary tells their friends of a big fight she and John had over breakfast. Mary says she hit John over the head with a tea kettle. John, in embarrassment, tried to 'soften the blow' and insisted that Mary actually hit him on the shoulder. Mary said on the head; John said on the shoulder, and so the battle was renewed. You don't have to tell everything you know.

Telling it all can be great fun or very threatening, depending on how secure you are. But what will people think? Remember, no one can diminish you without your permission. Others may even admire your courage and be inspired to communicate with you without barriers. But again – be appropriate.

I am always inspired by people's integrity. We have a friend who recently retired as president of a very large international corporation. He tells the story of his life openly. He left home in the midst of the depression with what little money his family could give him safety-pinned to his long underwear. He hitchhiked to find work, and rode for miles on the running boards [3] of nine cars. I am inspired by this man's honesty and openness.

Our pretenses shut us down and limit our growth and discovery. I often advise students at our department's annual orientation:

---

[3] Early model cars had an exterior panel along the doors which one stepped on to get in and out of the car.

*Be stupid! We all are at some level. Ask until you
understand. Don't pretend to know something –
that way you don't have to pretend you know or
defend what you know. You can be free to learn
and grow. If you think you know it all, then you
will not learn what you need to know.*

Another benefit of self-disclosure is that when you let
people know who you are, you release reactive energy. We carry
an emotional charge about what we must keep concealed.
When you disclose, you perceive fewer threats or attacks, and
you find less need to react irresponsibly to others.

A friend of mine was having bridgework done on her
front upper teeth and was worried about the results. After several visits to her dentist, she remained dissatisfied and went
directly to the laboratory. Her dentist became upset about this,
and she felt intimidated. She could have hidden her feelings,
but instead she told her dentist how she felt in a responsible
way: "I feel upset and intimidated by you." Immediately her
dentist was understanding and completed the process to her
satisfaction.

Take a moment to discover who you are. Find something,
anything, you are concerned about that is not OK about you.
Now look again and possibly accept it or place it in a new perspective. Notice your fear of what people will think. Notice that
if you can express your "not OK-ness," share or disclose it,
eventually you will lose the charge. For a period in my life, I
often compared myself to others whose brilliance I admired.
I grew to have a fear that I was stupid. I finally realized that it

was OK to be stupid, that all of us are in one way or another. Now I can tell anyone that story, and remarkably I rediscovered my own brilliance.

> *Because the Self is common to everyone, we all*
> *have the potential to be aware of our real inner*
> *natures.*
>
> — Peter Russell

What is your relationship with yourself? It is the basis for all the other relationships. The ego's identity constantly shifts in response to different persons and situations. Because the ego doesn't know itself, it is always in fear and doubt. It is constantly changing as it seeks approval or control and is always searching but never finding its true identity. In contrast, true-Self knows itself. It is a loving being often masked by the ego's fear or anger, but is never changing in its source.

Ask yourself repeatedly, "Who am I?" I am a professor; I am a husband; I am a father; I am a person. Sometimes I am ugly; sometimes I am loving. I choose to be loving. I am a loving being, regardless of my mistakes.

Special Relationships

The Romantic Kind
Ego's Illusion
You've found *the one*! The one you dreamed you could not live without. You could not believe the moment would ever come when this love could disappear. Yet it did. The beauty and excitement are gone, and in fact you are sick of and bored with

the one, and you would like to escape. You would have to make too many changes in *the one.* You made a mistake. Surely the one who could make you happy is still out there. You need to start searching again.

Where did the relationship go wrong? To find out let's carefully study how romantic relationships work. Why would you seek such a relationship in the first place? What do you really want in a romantic relationship? How about happiness? Really, don't most of us simply want someone who will make us happy? Isn't that essentially what it's all about? We often experience ourselves as incomplete or in need of a special relationship to make us happy because we live in fear and loneliness. Whatever the form the ego's need may take, we feel that need must be fulfilled to be happy. Our egos always seek the solutions externally. Thus, through our egos, we seek a relationship to meet our needs to make us happy. Simple, isn't it.

You found *the one to make you happy. The one* was perfect, beautiful, never lost his or her temper, was so this and so that. You did not consciously realize your decision, yet your message was clear, "Your responsibility for the rest of your life is to make me happy, and if you do, I will love you." Yet in an instant of sanity, you could see the job could be far more difficult than either of you might realize. You tried to find happiness on your own, and you failed. Obviously you need someone else to make you happy, and it's up to the other person to do it.

Ah! The problem is starting to surface. You may not have made it clear to *the one* exactly what his/her assignment was in the relationship. Oh, no! You don't suppose *the one* did the same with you. It could be he/she gave you the same assignment! And did he/she realize what was involved? Oh, and there was another part of the bargain you didn't explain:

> You better not screw up! I am giving you my most important assignment, 'Make me happy.' So if you screw up, I will be disappointed and unhappy, and if that happens, I will blame you and get angry and make you feel guilty for whatever you did or didn't do, say, or feel.

When *the one* makes you happy or unhappy, your ego voice interprets that your happiness is under someone else's control. Your ego projects your feelings to *the one* so you don't have to be responsible. When you look to another for your own validation and happiness, you feel incapable, unworthy, and impotent in the relationship. With or without awareness, you also feel resentment, anger, and guilt toward the one who "controls" your completeness and validation.

Your relationship has now become an entanglement. Thus, you find inexcusable, intolerable, unforgivable problems with *the one.* Your ego voice tells you that you must escape at any cost from the one who was the answer to your dreams and now has become the beginning of your nightmare. You must find another who is worthy, who can handle the job, who is capable of making you happy. Good luck!!!

The ego's special relationships never result in satisfaction because they always contain fear. Those persons who are the most "special" to us are a potential threat if we need their approval, validation, or security. Thus, we always fear loss or disapproval in special relationships. The ego's special object never receives unconditional love. Instead, a special relationship is an ego trip on another person. Special relations are the ego's answer to your loneliness and the incompleteness. Thus, a special relationship is the illusion of love.

Communication

Romantic relationships occur through mutual exploration in which each person releases more and more protective barriers by self-disclosure. We call this process getting to know each other. Indeed getting to know each other also involves getting to know yourself as well. Usually, we put most of our attention on physical and sexual barriers. Sexual behavior or communication is consummated through an experience of communion or at-oneness with another human being. Love by sexual communication and intimacy, however, is not lasting. The magic in the relationship seems to end when you get to know your mate as well as you apparently know yourself. The irony of this conclusion is that you may not know yourself at all let alone know the other person. As two people get to know each other, their intimacy loses its miraculous nature, and mutual antagonism, disappointments, and boredom may be all that's left after the initial excitement (Fromm). Now you must look for another to recreate that magic you once knew. To keep the excitement alive and to end the problems, a flow of marriages and divorces may seem necessary in your futile search to find the one to make you happy.

Most communication in a relationship reflects concepts and expectations of how men and women, husbands and wives, should be. Men should be ambitious, worldly, successful, and intelligent. They are to be strong, firm and magnanimous, and free of frailty and lesser emotions. Our society gives men the right to explore, discover, and express themselves. They have the opportunity for full self-expression.

Many women are rebelling against concepts and traditions that society has historically imposed: A woman's place is in the home. "Women should be mothers and homemakers only." "Women should be obedient to their husbands," etc. Women now have to choose from three alternatives: resignation to precast roles, rebellion against tradition, or full responsible expression of choice. Notice that the first two alternatives amount to suppression or reaction and result in stress. Only the third alternative offers freedom. Homemaking can be a cop-out or a beautiful career. So can a profession.

And so the illusory search for love and happiness continues in which we completely overlook the only source, namely, one's self. As long as you reach out for love and happiness, they will escape you. When you realize that you generate these experiences from within, you can obtain them in proportion to your willingness and ability to give.

There Is Another Way

A wonderful opportunity is available in every relationship. The miracle is yours by choosing a relationship as a basis to support and nurture each other's Self-discovery, for one can come to know another only through the knowledge of one's Self. Courage is required to extend freedom and support to another to learn and grow. True-Self extends its love to all creatures of the universe and does not limit itself to a special few the ego says it can possess. Through love, relationships are abundant because relationships can extend to many, in fact, potentially to everyone. And you can choose a special one.

Stewart Emery in his book, *Actualizations*, presents a discussion on romantic relationships. He states, "In a romantic relationship, what you really want from the other person is a more joyful experience of yourself. You will say 'I love you' if you experience yourself as joyful, lovable, capable in that person's presence, and that is exactly what your lover wants from you." Emery describes being in love as experiencing and expressing one's essence and supporting the other person to do the same: "Thus, love is when you are concerned with the other person's relationship with his or her own life rather than with your relationship to yours."

Marriage can be based on mutual support and expression, or merely on ego survival. Typical marriages contain both features. Society considers a successful marriage to be one in which both husband and wife compromise their very experience of aliveness for comfort and safety. My sense of a successful marriage is that each partner supports the other to reach their utmost ambition and potential. This process of becoming requires not only real love and courage but is also the only basis for freedom in a relationship.

Parent-Child Relationships

The constant cycle of parent-child relationships is one of nature's most remarkable unfoldings. Acceptance of this relationship is a beautiful opportunity for mutual validation, support, and growth for parents and children. In wholesome circumstances, the birth of a child can be a wonderful occasion. However, in the wrong circumstances it can be a tragedy. Astoundingly, we have yet to grasp the nature of child rearing as a profound responsibility.

Parents think they know, of course, by virtue of being graced as parents what is best for their child. They believe this has no egocentric motive. And what kind of a child would it be were *"its"* purpose not to make *"its"* parents proud? "Make us proud of you."

Pride takes many subtle forms. For example, a young mother told me she was ready to take her daughter to a rehearsal for a school play when upon looking at her daughter she said, "Oh, you can't go like this. Your nails are dirty, and your hair is a mess." To the mother's chagrin, her daughter replied, "Oh Mother, I was feeling so good about myself until you said that.""But what will people think of *me*, if *you* are not neat and clean?" said the mother. Cleanliness is fine, yet that was not the issue. Heaven forbid, our children should ever embarrass us! Pride is so pervasive. Act the right way, look the right way, join a proud profession, be a success or marry well. Then we justify what we want in the name of our child's happiness. The ego seeks control and appearances but strongly resists growth and discovery. Do you sense there could be conflict ahead?

> *Your children are not your children. They are*
> *the sons and daughters of Life's longing for itself.*
> *They come through you but not from you.*
> *And though they are with you, yet they belong*
> *not to you.* — Kahlil Gibran

Parents in the early phase of their child's life see themselves as unchallenged providers and protectors, and children in their innocence project perfection and omnipotence to parents. Parents and child experience an "unconditional love" in the mutually shared experience of innocence and perfection (Fromm). The child totally depends on its mother for nurturing, feeding, and well-being. Indeed, this is a real condition of the child's survival in the physical universe.

A child's early communication is primarily egocentric, for it knows only of its own wants and needs. The young child develops an imaginary world in its play and relationships (Piaget). For example, preschool children often play with imaginary friends and objects and talk out loud to and for them. As the parent-child relationship matures and expands, imperfections are learned and projected to self and others, and the relationship between parents and child loses the trust and innocence it once had. The child learns that to maintain parental love and support, she/he must conform to parental wishes. Parents become critical, and children become resentful or rebellious. Both use communication for the ego's purpose to control or seek acceptance.

A child eventually becomes independent of his parents, and through seeing their imperfections, becomes critical of them. The parents may suffer remorse, rejection, resentment, and self-consciousness about their own imperfections as highlighted by their children. The role between parent/child may then be reversed, as confounded by the ego. Although the relationship always extends from true-Self and love, the ego frequently is the apparent victor.

Ego Assignments:

a. As seen by the parents: fulfillment of parental images or ambitions (justified by the parental wisdom of what is best for the child).

b. As seen by the child: "The reason I turned out the way I did."

Parents establish most of the early *programming* of the child through their communication. Consequently, the child develops a personality that unconsciously manifests the many behavior patterns of his/her parents.

> *Personality is our most enduring trance state.*
> — William B. Arndt, Jr.

> *Parents are our first teachers and our first*
> *models.*   — Marilyn Ferguson

Parental communication, spoken and unspoken, often establishes pervasive and unconscious patterns in the child. We are imbued with parental expectations and fears. The latter often is communicated by unspoken injunctions of the parents' own fears and anxieties. Personality is a heritage bequeathed from generation to generation, strongly based on fear of failure, losing, being inferior, and what people will think; the result is insecurity and our communication reflects it.

Children, when uncontaminated by parental expectations and fears, are beautifully spontaneous and without judgment. Communication from innocence and detachment is honest; children tell anyone anything. Notice that when children do that, others accept their communication. It is natural expression. "Why don't you have any hair on your head?" "Grandma takes out her teeth at night," "You look funny," or "Billy was mean to me." Children are simply who they are (true-Self) and say what is so for them. Let me cite some true to life experiences of a family I know. Only their names are fictitious:

> Unus took her daughter, Clonus, to visit Grandma. Clonus said, "Grandma, I like the kind of cookies that you don't bake" (store bought cookies).

The child's experience of herself/himself may be profoundly influenced by his/her relationships. Communication with others is dyadic (i.e., an interaction in which one person is influenced by the other). Children naturally empower their parents and look to that source for approval and love. The nature of the parental feedback may greatly influence the child's expression. In general, if the child's communication is accepted and supported, his/her communication will flow spontaneously, and the child will feel secure. If the child's communication is rejected, corrected, and criticized, the child probably will feel suppressed and react from fear and insecurity. Suppressed communication is a loss of Self-power. Parents frequently are unconscious of their profound influence on their children.

> Borus was doing magic tricks for his three-year-old daughter, Clonus. Borus was making a number of small objects disappear. He told

Clonus that it was magic and boastfully said he could make anything disappear. With that, Clonus said, "Daddy disappear the TV! Disappear the TV!" Clonus was truly expectant and, needless to say, deeply disappointed.

As the child's communication becomes socialized from shoulds and shouldn'ts, do's and don'ts, corrections, expectations, and criticisms, the natural beauty, innocence, and spontaneity of childhood diminishes. The child's expression, influenced by fear and guilt, is withheld or replaced by covert egocentric communications. By the time the child enters school, her/his speech goes underground. Children normally express themselves aloud in speech until that period, and then the egocentric speech becomes covert, or silent, inner speech (Vygotsky). The child learns he/she is no longer free to talk aloud when and where he/she chooses, because such expression may no longer be safe or acceptable. I believe this is the basis of the ego voice that I described in Chapter III.

In his book, *Between Parent and Child*, Dr. Haim Ginott describes communication that children use to explore their relationships. They become precocious experts in hidden messages. Children may fear abandonment. A three-year-old may say, "Daddy, Susan's father doesn't come home any more. You won't leave me, will you?" By age seven she may have become covert, "Susan's father moved away. Daddy, do you think that you would ever move away?" Children start to use "what if" questions to mask their personal situations. Look for the hidden meaning.

Parents continuously try to solve or react to the communication of their children rather than understand their meaning and feelings. Carl came home from the Little League baseball game in tears. He hated his coach and was never going to play again. The problem was that the coach had put another player in the game in Carl's place. Carl's mother immediately lectured him, "You have to do what the coach (and others as well) say in life, and you better get used to it. What about the other boys? Shouldn't they get to play, too?"

Carl's mother missed the point. He already knew what she told him in her lecture. Let's try another response: "You are disappointed, aren't you? I really understand how you feel." Respond to the feelings, the communication – don't give the rule book. The child already knows the way it is.

The typical communication between parent and child is parental authority, expectations, and manipulation of the child. Children learn, all too often, that they must be and talk a certain way to be safe or accepted by their parents. "Don't tell the truth about who you are and how you feel." "Don't use bad words even though parents do." Not only does communication become stilted, but so does the relationship. The child evolves an act – a false self – an ego to hide behind, because who they really are is apparently not OK.

Role playing usually is by words and not example in our parent-child communication, and its outcome is dishonesty in the communication and the relationship. Eventually children, as teenagers, may rebel against authority and expectations of the relationship because much of this authority is based on misperception and deception.

Parents often deceive themselves by apparently noble justification: "I want you to have a college education so you can be happy and successful." Is it important for your child to go to college? Sociologists tell us that formal education has little to do with happiness. Discuss the matter honestly. "Do you want to go to college? Why? Why not?" A famous humorist once commented that "I doubt that a college education would hurt anyone who has normal intelligence."

Consider expectations that were set up for you, and the expectations you set up for your children. Parents often control their children to avoid their own fears and disappointments, or to have their children look successful as a reflection of the family ego. You must search for the bottom line to discover the truth about your motivation. The ego does not state the truth so look to your intuitive voice. Some friends discovered their son was about to flunk out of a university. His mother became fearful and protective and was prepared to pull strings or whatever was necessary to save her son from failure. "What shall we do?" she asked her husband. He replied compassionately, "Let him figure it out."

"True compassion," said one spiritual teacher, "is ruthless." Or, as the poet Guillaume Apollonaire put it:

Come to the edge, he said.
We are afraid, they said:
Come to the edge, he said.
They came.
He pushed them . . . and they flew.

The father could have submitted to his wife's fear to pull

strings to return his son to college. But who would that really serve, the parents or the child? Children need true, honest parental love and support, yet real courage and compassion are required to let the youthful learn on their own. Children will reach out and discover themselves as we give them our love, support, and compassion. They will explore and discover and expand.

And reciprocally, children are their parents' teachers. Are you willing to learn from your children? Are you open to their communication and contribution to you? Children have much to contribute to their parents, but "when the shoe is on the other foot," parents often are resistant and defensive. Each generation creates a new reality through communication, and you can grow with it; you can empower yourself and your children by receiving and understanding their communication.

Friendship

What are friends for? Friends are to invite you to come to parties, to go to special events, or to visit extraordinary places. Friends should be interesting, entertaining, and exciting. Friends should celebrate your successes, sympathize with your failures, and be there for you when things go wrong. They should say the right thing at the right time and forgive you for your shortcomings and errors even if you don't forgive them. And certainly they should conform to your standards, your moral and social values and practices, and to your lifestyle as well.

Clearly, we must select our friends carefully if they are to respond to our wishes and fulfill our wants and needs. I hope this "advice" doesn't sound too self-centered or egotistic, but then, what are friends for? Friends can help us enhance our image and our reputation, and help us to succeed in the world. It is vitally important then to know the right people and to have the right friends. After all, others will judge us by our friends. If you have the right friends, and if you can drop the right names, doors will open, and you can climb the social ladder. You too can enter influential circles; you too can become one of the elite! People will envy your social standing and "power." Then you will know that you have arrived and attained your role in the American dream!

What is the conventional wisdom regarding friendship? We are taught to believe that "it's not what you know, but who you know that counts." If you know the right people, they can enhance your achievement of success in the world. Then you will feel important. But if you are not "born" into success, "it" can be hard to get, but not impossible. If you are a "have not," then hang out with the "haves" and fake it, and you will at least be accorded this aura in the eyes of those who don't know the difference. Whether you are a "have" or a "have not," you will feel like you have arrived, and actually that is all there is to it. In fact, the whole trip reduces to a state of mind and chosen values. What is it then that we are searching for in the name of friendship?

Let us take inventory. What is it you seek in your friends? What kind of friends have you chosen and why have you chosen them? Ask yourself also, why they have chosen you? Look to see if you have any motives or constraints that limit or preclude your communication. If so, what are your investments?

What are your motives? Then ask yourself, is there a hidden agenda? Whatever your conclusions, you need not withdraw or renounce the friendship, you need only transform your relationship with yourself. Do your friends buy into your melodrama and reinforce it by ego agreement, or do they support you to be honest and responsible, and to seek within to discover who you are? How then should we proceed?

Ego involvement results in hollow, diminishing or short-lived friendships, but there is another way: friendship, as seen by the true-Self is a discovery of mutual respect, empathy, and power that exists between, actually within, yourself and others regardless of worldly values, achievements, or status. For example, the great gift of the Dalai Lama of Tibet is his ability to communicate this message potentially to everyone he meets, and practically everyone he meets gets his message. He does not see himself as special in any way. Were he to do so, he would sacrifice all real and lasting power. What people fail to recognize, however, is that the beauty, love, and power that they experience in the presence of the Dalai Lama does not come from the Dalai Lama; it comes from within each one of them because they have opened their true-Self to him.

Friendship is nothing special or perhaps everything special. Friendship is simply being friendly, expressing your mutual respect and love and joy to each person you meet. This is the great greeting ritual and symbol of the Hindus, expressed by the prayerful gesture of the hands clasped vertically over the lips, and the expression, "Namasté," through which each one acknowledges another in profound respect and humility.

A similar greeting exists in Buddhism and is described

as "Loving Kindness." The good Samaritan creed is another expression: "Do unto others as you would have others do unto you." How many times have I, and perhaps you, failed to exercise this fundamental awareness. Yet let me also offer encouragement; we both shall be given another opportunity. What we all need is to practice, so go in peace, shalom.

True friendship can only be expressed by those who are self-aware (an awareness of being whole and complete) and who express oneness between two apparently separate beings. Friendship is an opportunity to discover your own inner power and love and to share it with another through your communication. Communication is the bridge. "Love your neighbor as yourself" could be rephrased as "Empower your neighbor as yourself." Friends can help us feel better about ourselves by reminding us quite humbly who we are. Actually, this is as good as it gets.

Being Number One

"So what would you like to be when you grow up?" If you are like many others, you may still be asking yourself that question every Monday morning. Have you ever awakened in the morning and wondered what it's all about and do you really matter anyway? Things would be different, you say, if you knew you had a purpose. What does the world value? What do we aspire to in our jobs? What do our parents and peers and our society value? Whatever it is, you can be sure that we are influenced by 'it' in no small way. So what is the conventional wisdom? What do we need to feel important?

I need to have more, get better, or be different. I could get a lot of money, one way or another, it matters not how. Or I could become a movie star. I could be rich and famous, then I could buy anything I wanted. People would solicit me for money, and I would be influential. Or I could enter a proud profession. I could become a medical doctor and save people's lives. I could have power over life and death. Wow, how important can you get! But maybe I wouldn't want to be a doctor and take care of sick people; I could become a lawyer or an executive. I could go into politics and become powerful. People would come to me for jobs and to do my bidding. And if they please me, I could give them special opportunities so that they would know my influence. That's it. That's the answer: I need to find something to make me feel important – to make me feel special – it doesn't matter what.

I have to do something that gives me power or authority. What it really boils down to – bottom line – is that I want to be the boss. Then I will be in charge. I will have a sense of power, and if all else fails, at least I will get my way. At least I want to be my own boss. If I can't tell others what to do, then at least I can be in charge of myself.

Do you get the feeling that you may have been set up for a big ego trip? Sure I know – that you know – that everybody knows – that what matters is that you are happy doing what you do. The job doesn't really matter if you are happy doing it. You don't even have to be the boss. But is that how we select our jobs?

I am reminded of the movie, *The Bridge on the River Kwai*, about imprisoned, brutalized British soldiers forced to build a bridge over a river to aid the Japanese army's advance in

Burma. The Japanese commander instructed the enslaved captives before each work day and his closing comment was always, "Be happy in your work." It would never have occurred to the British prisoners that they actually had a choice. How could anyone be happy in his work under such circumstances? But ironically their commander (Alec Guinness) proceeded to build a magnificent structure with great pride and joy and to the amazement of his men! Are you happy in your work? Maybe it has not occurred to you that you actually have a choice.

In my work I have noticed that I am both *employee and boss*. This may sound like the best (or worst) of both worlds. Yet, at some level of relationship, everyone is both. Even at the top you must be responsive to subordinates if you wish to be successful. You can't fire everyone. And if you are low man on the totem pole, you are still the boss in your relationship to your job. Each of us is an employee and each of us is a boss in whatever we decide to do.

Determine how you are an employee in your job. Clearly, if a president, even of his own private company, does not relate to and effectively serve employees and customers, he will fail. Who is freer, the employee or the boss? It may simply depend on how you look at it, for being either one or the other is more a matter of concept than something you know from experience.

Looking at your work this way also affords a valuable perception. If you envision yourself as both an employee and a boss, you can determine that both positions need to be supported.

Ego's Game

The ego's game of being important – or being the boss – seems to be a popular one to play. But does it really lead to satisfaction? And is its value real or just imagined? Ego would have you be boss because it imagines that your job should make you feel important. But just in case you are not the boss, it holds a consolation prize. You get to be the boss's chief critic. Thus, whatever might displease your ego, the boss will get the blame. So you assume another source of power. You are the one who knows what should be done: "Now if I were the boss, things would be different." That way you think you share your grief and distinguish your inherent superiority.

In all walks of life, people complain and criticize from their own feelings about themselves: resentment, jealousy, resistance to authority; and they pay the price through their own dissatisfaction. Honest and responsible disagreements are not manifested in these ways. If you want something, say so. Usually, what is between you and what you want may be pride, fear of rejection or invalidation, fear of failure and, even fear of success.

Your ego voice may lead you into three common traps: 1) taking your job personally – if you don't get the promotion, don't take it personally; 2) threatening or blaming the boss (this is a good way to start a feud or get fired); and 3) lack of fairness—we hate to accept that life is not fair. You don't have to like the fact that life is unfair, but resenting unfairness is a trap. For example, one person is in charge of a project, and he does the job well. He hires a new assistant. The assistant is good, but he and the project director don't work well together.

Perhaps their differences can be arbitrated, but let's say they can't. Who has to go? Is it fair? The boss often cannot be fair when fairness is not the issue. We are taught to be fair in our society, but fairness is a concept that is exercised by an opinion; it does not exist in reality.

True-Self

> *When we experience the power of the Self, there is an absence of fear, there is no compulsion to control, and no struggle for approval or external power.*

> — Deepak Chopra

When ego dominates in employees or bosses, both sides lose the game. You inherit grief and dissatisfaction. There is a better way. True-Self knows that it is employee and boss, and neither wins the battle unless each supports the other. True-Self extends power to others. Those who know true power, give it away, and are more empowered in return. As the student empowers the master, so the employee empowers the boss. When you empower the boss, you empower yourself. You become bigger than your ego's petty ways. You experience being OK with yourself, and others may experience it too.

We have all seen the drama of those who would sacrifice everything for money, power, and influence, yet end up in disillusionment and dissatisfaction. It is the story of the young executive who makes it to the top only to quit his job to look for satisfaction. There is a delightful book about getting to the top called *Hope for the Flowers* (Paulus). It describes the process of getting there and the subsequent need to keep a structure in place for fear you might fall.

You are not your job. You are your Self. If you are not committed to your job, then eventually you will lose it. If you dislike your job, only insecurity and fear justify keeping it. If you can't support or change an organization, or if you can't support its purpose, find a purpose you can support. There are always opportunities for those who have courage and want to contribute. And it's not the job; it is what you bring to it that matters. Quit if you choose, but if you stay, play the game with a full commitment, or you will become angry and frustrated. The nature of the job, believe it or not, really doesn't matter. "But I save lives," the ego might demand! Yes, don't we all, if we choose responsibility.

Work is love expressed. But what about the boss? True-Self as boss empowers others. Powerful people empower others. Are you willing to be responsible as a leader? Are you willing to communicate clear agreements between you and your fellow workers and exercise mutual commitments? It is no small matter. It requires active participation and communication and full acknowledgment of others.

Being a good leader can be a tough job because supporting others includes being at risk. Will you honestly and directly appraise others' performance, or will you hide behind your own unworthiness? Will you let others experience the results of their own performance? What if the job does not get done? Clearly, if your employees are bus drivers who don't get to work on time or scientists who never complete or publish their experiments, you can spend only so much time supporting them. A tough job perhaps, but a boss must discharge those who need to learn to keep their agreements, and who can't work with others. Growth is painful without responsibility.

A leader must be responsible. If you know who you are, you need not justify yourself to one who does not assume responsibility. Compassion is love expressed to one who needs to learn the lesson of responsibility. If you protect others from the consequences of their own actions or their inaction, you are actually protecting yourself. You provide a hiding place to avoid responsibility (called enabling) and that is <u>not</u> a loving thing to do. If you do not exercise responsibility as boss, you may not keep the job.

> *A dictator is not a true leader because he is not*
> *open to the input of his followers.*
> — Marilyn Ferguson

We are not qualified to judge other human beings because we don't know why they behave as they do. Judge instead their performance. Do they do their job or not? Failure is not proof of anything; it is another opportunity to discover who you are. What might appear to be failure may lead to an opportunity to learn and grow. Success and failure are both illusions of the ego. Mistakes are opportunities for learning.

Incomplete Relationships (Including Those Departed)

Let's say you had an upset or incomplete communication with someone who has moved away or with someone who has died. You may feel regret, guilt, anger, or resentment regarding this person. Yet the person is no longer available to you to resolve these feelings. Apparently then, you must live with these feelings the rest of your life. If I stated that you could resolve your communication with someone who has since departed this world, you might really become alarmed. Do not be concerned; there is no hocus-pocus, ouji-boards, or seance about this. Actually no magic or supernatural feats are necessary.

Just examine the facts. Let's say your Aunt Tilly died, and you owed her money that you purposely avoided repaying her. You surely can't send her the money or for that matter, ask her forgiveness. But look again, Aunt Tilly has passed on. She doesn't want the money now, and you can't experience her forgiveness. In other words, at this point, Aunt Tilly doesn't have a problem, but apparently you do. You still have unhappy feelings, yet you project them to Aunt Tilly. You are all you are dealing with. Forgive yourself — only you can free yourself from your own self-condemnation and guilt. The problem and the solution can only be found in your mind.

Select Your Own Assignments

We operate from a split mind in our relationships. Relationships serve to enable one to discover one's true-Self or to seek an identity by pursuing the ego's illusions. True-Self knows itself and extends love and truth. Ego knows not what it is, thus seeks an identity for itself. The real you is lost in the ego's identity. The ego uses relationships only to meet its needs. The ego has an assignment for each relationship it has. Ego must control others in relationships to get what it wants. It uses anger to make others feel guilty in an attempt to control them.

True-Self accepts and supports others in expressing themselves and in learning what they seek to learn. There is only one issue in all relationships: that others accept you the way you are. And that is all others want from you. Ironically, we want to be accepted as we are, but we have a design for how everyone else should be. Others must change the way they are in order to gain our acceptance or approval. The very thing we insist upon for ourselves, we will not grant to others.

The bottom line in relationships is acceptance. If you want peace, support, and love in your relationships, say "yes" to what is. Surrender your control of others and let them be themselves. This also grants freedom for yourself.

> *We are all interconnected and help bring one*
> *another into the expression of our*
> *full potential through words, thoughts and deeds*
> *that are unimaginable in their simplicity and*
> *untraceable in their complexity.*
> — Joan Borysenko

It has become apparent that communication is the key to love and power, relationships, self-empowerment and healing. For the final chapter we will consider communication as the pathway to personal transformation.

Chapter Eight Insights
Relationships: A Mirror of Yourself

1. We live in a world of perceptions and judgments. Explain both proper and improper use of judgments.

2. Indicate a special relationship (friend, parent, etc.)
   a. Describe the role you have given this person.
   b. What is your response to them when they fail to do your bidding?
   c. How do you try to control them?
   d. How does trying to control others also imprison you?

3. Identify an interaction or relationship that is incomplete or is not working for you.
   a. What is there in that interaction that you are not communicating?
   b. What is keeping you from communicating it?
   c. Indicate what you need to do or communicate to clear up that interaction.

4. Describe how your relationships are a mirror of how you see yourself.

5. What do you need to do to heal your relationship with others?

CHAPTER NINE

A Transformative Vision

Good News, Bad News

Let's look at the bad news first to see what we are up against; then let's look at the good news to discover our astounding and unlimited potential. Thus we can play the game of life with a full deck, and we can pursue our goals with a realistic perspective.

The bad news is that life is difficult and this is a tough world to live in. It is a challenging place and ultimately nobody survives it. Life is full of difficult lessons, and given our conditioned learning and our egocentric minds, most of us learn the lessons of life the hard way. Also, our ego-mind is not a good teacher; in fact, it is a trickster (like Wily Coyote), and its way of looking at life is amazingly deceptive.

The ego poses as good news, but behind its worldly attractions, the ego conceals its bad news. For example, the ego tells us how to achieve many worldly goals and acquisitions to gain self-esteem and happiness; however, it fails to point out to us that our *ego-trips* also lead to conflict, guilt, fear, and stress, and that in the end its victories are never completely satisfying. For example, recall our earlier discussion about our ego's quest to find someone, a special person, to make us happy. Did the one selected ever really get the job done completely to your ego's satisfaction? The ego also neglects to point out to us that all of the things that we gain and cherish in our lives on planet earth, sooner or later, will be taken away.

But do not despair because there is good news, and it is quite marvelous indeed! Fortunately, there is another Self or mind (i.e., way of thinking) that offers an alternative to the ego.

This Self represents a spiritual self and an unconditioned, natural state of mind that is whole and complete and that is the experience of unconditional peace, love, and joy. This Self (or mind) is one with all other minds. How can this be? Minds are joined by ways of thinking. The Self, or unconditional mind, is joined or unified by its spirituality and its belief in oneness (i.e., that beyond the body, we are joined by unconditional love). Again, minds are joined when they share a common way of thinking. Only minds can join. Bodies are always separate.

There Are Two "Selves"

There are two different ways of thinking. In Chapter One I described the ego conditioned mind as a false self. However, I also introduced in Chapter Two another mind or another Self, which I call true-Self. This true, or spiritual Self, or unconditional mind, believes in oneness. Consequently, it is internally dependent and experiences itself as whole and complete. Conversely, the ego-self believes in separation. As a result, the ego-self is externally dependent and experiences itself as alienated and incomplete.

The Self experiences itself as whole and complete; the ego experiences itself as alienated and incomplete, and the mind sees others as it sees itself. Recall from our discussion on relationships that how we see others is a mirror of our own mind. We have learned from the time of birth to identify with our ego-self and are profoundly conditioned to believe that the ego's world, its values, and its way of thinking reflects our reality; however, it is important to realize that the release of the ego leads not to oblivion, but rather to self-awareness. We must choose one mind or the other because these minds are mutually exclusive. Choose we must, and this discovery and realization – this need to choose – starts us on the journey of mental and/or spiritual healing.

The Journey
Healing is a journey, not a destination. We are all on the challenging journey of life, hopefully to empowerment and healing, regardless of the pathway we choose to take. But what do we do? How do we get there from here? From one point of view, there is nothing to do – just release the ego. But from another point of view, we are absolutely overwhelmed by our egocentric conditioning and existence. What a paradox!

Is our struggle over? Or is it just beginning? There is no simple answer. But let's not give up too quickly. As the great baseball player, Yogi Berra, used to say, "It ain't over 'til it's over."

The experience of life on Earth is challenging and may seem overwhelming. The American way, of course, is to discover a quick fix or find a magic bullet. The fact is – there is no magic solution! Our ego world is caught in never ending strife:

conflict, guilt, fear, stress, disease, and violence, and there is no quick fix. We must find an alternative, and that aspect of the journey is up to each one of us. No one can do it for us.

In the movie *Gandhi,* there is a scene in which a Moslem man who had murdered a Hindu child in revenge for the murder of his own child confronts Gandhi. In guilt, grief, and despair, the Moslem man begs Gandhi to help him. Gandhi very thoughtfully and compassionately responds, "I know a way out of hell for you." Gandhi then offers his healing balm or potion. He tells the Moslem man to adopt a Hindu child, the age of his own son who was murdered by a Hindu, and to rear his adopted child as a Hindu. This is a beautiful and powerful idea, but let us not miss the most critical point. In effect, Gandhi advised this guilty and grief stricken Moslem man to heal his relationship with Hindu people by rearing his adopted child as Hindu. The Moslem man was provided a pathway – a journey – to heal his relationship with himself. Remember – our relationships are a mirror of our own minds or ways of thinking.

I have come to recognize that Gandhi's realization and advice to the Moslem man is my lesson too, and perhaps it is your lesson as well. Could it just be that Gandhi's astounding wisdom is exactly what is wanted and needed in this harsh world of ours? Could it just be that this lesson, this need to heal our relationships, is what each one of us is seeking? Remember, our relationships are our mirror, our reflection of our inner self. This is our lesson – our journey – on planet Earth. Let us pursue our journey to healing. However, this is not an easy journey. We need to empower ourselves in order to experience healing. The journey, therefore, is to heal our relationships; they are our mirrors. However, the journey both starts and ends with healing our self. Have you not already discovered that this is the most critical aspect of our lives?

Permit me to identify two major problems: First, although most people experience considerable pain and suffering in their lives, from family strife to wars, for the most part, people do not know there is an alternative, that there is another way.

And secondly and more significantly, all people are profoundly, egocentrically conditioned and have an enormous investment in their ego. Thus we must proceed with an open mind and experiment and evaluate for ourselves.

Be True To Your Self

The true-Self always seeks inner guidance. We simply have no idea how strongly invested we are in the ego. Our egocentric world appears to be our reality, and we seem to have the proof in our experiences. So what can we do? First notice that you have an alternative. Look on the ego's judgments and defenses with an unconditional mind – with full conscious awareness – and with unconditional love. Remember what appears to the ego as an attack can be seen by the Self as a call for help. What appears to ego as fear and anger or hate and revenge can be seen by the Self as a call for love (ACIM).

However, be appropriate in the situation; self-empowerment is not pacifistic. For example, in certain situations, if violence is threatened or occurs, calling the police may be the best action to take. It is not loving to any person – to the victim or to the victimizer or to an observer – to overlook attack or to abandon one's sense of responsibility. As mentioned earlier, our ego existence is a tough place to be. So what can we do? In every situation go within; follow your inner guidance. Be true to your Self.

Countless people have been greatly influenced, even amazed, by pacifists like Buddha, Socrates, Jesus, Gandhi, Dr. Martin Luther King, and others who have suffered physical abuse to themselves, and even endured the murder of loved ones and followers. Yet these pacifists abstained from violent reactions. Indeed, such courage, commitment, and selflessness are astounding.

However, I am greatly perplexed by the thought that "true" pacifists, by definition, cannot ever use physical force and would stand by "peacefully" while someone violently attacked helpless, innocent victims. Does this mean that "true" pacifists would stand aside and watch the "Stalins" and "Adolph Hitlers" dominate and terrorize humanity? What if a police or peace officer stood "peacefully by" and watched the murder of others, perhaps even school children? What would you think? How would you feel?

I consider myself a pacifist; however, I view pacifism in a larger perspective. I believe that meaning is ultimately determined by purpose. Violence, therefore, is ultimately a state of mind resulting from intentions and feelings, what we mean when we say, "where you are coming from." For example, as young teenage boys, my best friend and I often engaged in boxing matches. From time to time, we would bruise the other's eye or bloody the other's nose, but our intentions were not violent. Regardless of the outcomes of our matches, the final "round" was always laughter, friendship for one another, and joy. There was nothing malicious or "hateful" in our intentions.

One may need to use physical force in self-defense, which may appear to lead to psychological conflict for one who pursues spiritual awareness and/or pacifism. However, violence can be seen as a state of mind, even as violent or non-violent communication (Rosenberg) is contingent on malicious versus protective intentions. Thus defensive physical action can be used without a sense of inner conflict.

The marvelous mythological tale of the Bhagavad Gita has always impressed me. Krishna, a magnificent Hindu god, challenges Arjuna, the great warrior-king, to counterattack his own relatives, who were on a violent rampage in the kingdom. "But I can't attack and kill my own relatives," pleads Arjuna, to which Krishna responds with his famous quote, "How can the immortal die?" Krishna then proceeds with another challenge, loosely restated by me, "Are you going to be king (do your duty, fulfill your dharma) or not?"

Then as Arjuna reviews his relatives' violence, he proclaims both in justification and anger, "Yes, I shall counterattack." Krishna then ironically restrains Arjuna, and in so many words asks, "Are you going to counterattack in anger and violence or from a sense of peace and responsibility? The first duty is peace of mind; the second is appropriate action."

Being profoundly impressed by the Gita, I have always said that I am not a pacifist because I do believe in self-defense, in law and order and in defending others if physical action is necessary. However, I would like to suggest pacifism is not an expression of behavior, but a state of mind.

As a more dramatic example, let me share a true experience of an older cousin of mine who, in a battle during World War II, found himself in a state of shock in the midst of an enemy attack. As he emerged from his state of shock, he resumed the battle, and based on his sense of responsibility to his comrades, he killed a number of "enemies," yet maintained a profound sense of calmness and fearlessness. At the same time, he felt compassion for his victims. While continuing "to destroy" the enemy, he became remarkably aware of the insanity that was taking place in the midst of battle; nevertheless, doing his duty, he continued to "destroy" the enemy. He subsequently completed his tour of duty without anger or hatred toward the enemy and later described this situation as the most profound experience of his life.

The use of the term "peace officer" has taken on a double meaning for me. One may need to use physical force to maintain the peace, to do one's duty in protecting one's self and others, but a true "peace officer" performs his duty, as Krishna admonished Arjuna, with a sense of responsibility in a state of peace. Therefore the ultimate goal for the pacifist must be *peace of mind.* Each of us may become a pacifist simply by choosing inner peace while still performing one's duties and responsibilities in life.

Empowerment and healing are not something that we achieve; they are natural states of the unconditional mind and Self. The ego is a barrier to this natural state of mind. What we must do is actually an "undoing" – a release – of our ego judgments or attacks. In this release, we return to our natural state of mind and Self.

Mistakes Are Stepping Stones

Mistakes can be seen as challenges and opportunities for learning. Healing is not an easy process. But then, as I noted above, if mistakes are truly opportunities, you will have an abundance of opportunities for practice. Conduct your own experiments in the laboratory of your mind. Healing is a process of making mistakes and learning from them. The trick is to learn from our mistakes as quickly as we can.

However, be wary of your ego defenses. Above all else, keep an open mind! As my father was fond of saying, "If you think you know, you have nothing to learn." Be a possibility thinker. Try it yourself and see if it works. Then you will have your own answer.

But this is not the way our ego-mind has been conditioned. We learned many lessons as children: We learned not to be there (i.e., we learned to be complacent and not to take responsibility). We learned to blame someone else. We also learned not to communicate, not to say what is really true for us, because we are likely to be corrected, shamed, or suppressed. We also very quickly learned to deny or to hide our mistakes. As a result, we have learned that it is safer to be in a stupor than to ask a question and reveal our ignorance. Thus we are cautious and reluctant to seek new experiences or to explore. What will people think or say about us! Let me make a suggestion. Don't worry about it; other people are too busy worrying about what others are thinking about them to be aware of you.

I have made countless mistakes. I am a slow learner and very purposefully so, although it seems that I have had to learn everything the hard way. However painful, this is often how our learning occurs. Look at the obvious – at what everyone takes for granted – take your time, be a slow learner, and you will be astounded at what everyone overlooks. The glib learner, the speed reader, the great memorizer, rarely really learns. Learning requires careful thought and understanding. If you do not find yourself reading and pondering, then you may have substituted memorization for learning. Believe me, there is a profound difference.

I want to prepare you for a challenging task so that you will not give up in discouragement. Self-empowerment and healing require that we learn to be whole and complete within ourselves, which is the hardest lesson to learn in life. You must learn this lesson if you wish to enter a world of unconditional love and joy.

The ego calls the external world the "real world." The rules are: "Dog eat dog," "every man for himself," "kill or be killed," "survival of the fittest," "don't get angry, get even," etc. This is fear – "paranoid schizophrenia" – a carryover to humanity from the primordial animal kingdom. There is another reality and it takes real courage, real power and wisdom, and a very mature and secure person to discover and share it. This is the real world, but it does not exist outside you. It exists within your Self.

Let us close this section with a practical example. A friend of mine, Roy, likes to compare controlling ego attacks to driving a car. When you are driving, notice that you keep the car under control simply by frequent minor adjustments of the steering wheel. However, if you overreact, then you increase the chances of the car going out of control. The same is true for the ego. If you get carried away with your ego judgments and over-react rather than own them, you are likely to "crash and burn." Learning to deal with your ego responsibly takes both patience and persistence.

Blazing A Trail: In Search Of The Self

There seems to be no way to get there from here. Each of us since childhood has been suppressed in many ways. We have been taught that mistakes lead to embarrassment or punishment. The child has her mouth washed out with soap for saying words in innocence because the parent's interpretation leads to shock or shame. An innocent child is punished for the parent's guilt. In public life, past mistakes may be used by the opposition to destroy one's hopes and career. Is a criminal ever viewed without his crimes? We all have been taught not to make mistakes. As a result, we become suppressed, cautious, and reluctant to seek new experiences and to explore. After all, "What will people think or say about us?"

Often, self-expression is not safe. Eventually we lose the energy, enthusiasm, and spontaneity of childhood. We often guard, withhold, or falsify our communication and expression, and we rationalize by saying that "it doesn't really matter." Perhaps the bottom line barrier to full self-empowerment and healing is a belief that what we do or say doesn't matter.

Each one of us wants to be special. We want to be right and to win. That is the essential feature of egocentricity. But we need not give up our desire to be special in order to become empowered and healed. Indeed, we can use this desire to motivate us. We need only change our purpose for being special from egocentricity to self-empowerment and healing. How then can we become special? We can teach what we need to learn. This sounds like a contradiction in terms, but it isn't. Perhaps the most beautiful, inspiring, and empowering aspect of healing is that in order to empower and heal your self, you must inherently share this process with others who may or may not accept it. So if you want to be special, empower and heal yourself and share your experience with others.

Let me share a well-known story with you. Although this story is reportedly untrue, we can use both its strengths and its weaknesses as an example to start us on our search. This is the story of the hundredth monkey (Keyes), which I have reinterpreted.

The Japanese monkey, *Macaca fuscata*, has been observed in the wild for over 30 years. In 1952 on the island of Koshima, scientists were providing monkeys with sweet potatoes dropped in the sand. The monkeys liked the taste of the raw sweet potatoes, but they found the dirt unpleasant. An 18 month-old female named Imo discovered that she could solve the problem by washing the potatoes in a nearby stream. She taught this method to her mother and also to her playmates who also taught their mothers too. This cultural innovation was gradually picked up by various monkeys before the eyes of scientists. All the young monkeys learned to wash the sandy sweet potatoes to make them more palatable. However, many of the adult monkeys ignored this innovation and kept eating the dirty sweet potatoes.

By analogy, we can learn to heal ourselves and to share our learning through our own practice. We teach what we need to learn. However, healing ourselves is not as simple as washing potatoes, and we will continue to make mistakes. But we can learn and teach how to use our mistakes as stepping stones. Clearly, whether others with whom we interact choose to learn and to teach empowerment and healing for themselves is entirely up to them. This leads me to the next point that I want to make.

The story of the hundredth monkey was then extended further, but erroneously. Supposedly the practice of washing sweet potatoes, when it was adopted by a critical mass (i.e., the hundredth monkey), jumped miraculously to monkeys located on distant islands.

Our ego is devoted to a belief that empowerment and healing will be achieved vicariously through others – through the great masters – who will do it for us. No doubt you have learned by now that no one can do this for you. The misperception arises from the ego that we are powerless and that everything – good or bad – just happens to us. The ego is not responsible.

This is the key weapon in the ego's arsenal to defend itself against the Self and against unconditional peace and love, which the ego sees as a threat to its survival. But do not be fearful. The Self does not attack. However, complacency is an ego strategy. Recall from Dante's *Inferno* – alluded to here strictly as an analogy – that the hottest places in hell are saved for the complacent.

Portrait Of A True Master

*Perfection isn't trying to be perfect; it's just
perfection.* (The natural state of one's true-Self)
— Susan Yarian

Let me depict our journey with a more gentle and loving brush. Being a master is ultimately a natural expression of mind or, an expression of our natural mind.

*To one who knows who he is,
no explanation is necessary.
To one who does not know who he is,
no explanation is possible.*
— Lao Tzu, *The Tao*

Let me give you an example. I have a very close companion who inspires me by his simplicity. He is himself at every moment and always expresses himself from that context. He is direct and honest about how he feels, regardless of what others may think about him. He rarely feigns an expression and is rarely covert. He is not encumbered by pride nor inhibited or withdrawn from embarrassment. Occasionally he may be reserved with unknown people, yet he opens himself completely when he senses the company is safe. He is lovingly spontaneous, although others from time to time may view him as inappropriate or intrusive. He is open to the expression of others and always understanding. He is reasonably responsive, yet exercises his own decisions, which frequently run counter to the wishes of even his closest friends. He is loyal, never undermines others, keeps his word, and never withholds his loving expression. He is a joyful companion and supportive teacher (and he does all this without words). He unpretentiously goes by the name of "Willy" – he is our pet poodle.

Meanwhile, Back At The Paradox

As stated previously under the heading **"Who Am I?"** we are whole and complete – already healed – in our natural or unconditional state of mind, which can be verified by the experience of unconditional peace, love, and joy. Yet, ironically, we find ourselves entrapped in our egocentric identity and our sense of alienation, resulting in an experience of conflict, guilt, fear, and stress. So here we are back at the paradox. How can this be?

Permit me to provide an analogy, actually a famous allegory, Plato's allegory of the cave. Imagine a group of prisoners chained to the wall of a cave in which they exist essentially in darkness. During certain very limited periods of the day, however, light permeates the cave sufficiently for the prisoners to see their shadows on the wall. This existence becomes so deeply ingrained in these prisoners that the shadows actually become their experience of reality. However, a particularly adventuresome and courageous prisoner frees himself from his chains and "enters the light" that permeates the cave to the outside world. He returns to the cave in jubilation to share his discovery of the true reality with his long suffering fellow prisoners. However, his fellow prisoners become so shocked and frightened by his offerings – light and freedom – that they turn on him and attack him.

But this, of course, is just an allegory – a story – and who could believe such a tale? Let's consider, an equally unbelievable story, but one that is based on a factual account. Many American, British, and Australian soldiers in the Philippines and other Pacific islands were captured during World War II and held in Japanese prison camps, and these prisoners endured both starvation and torture during several years of captivity. Fortunately, near the end of the war the survivors of these prison camps were liberated by their comrades. To the amazement of their liberators, however, the prisoners were terrified to leave the prison. They had come to accept it as their security, and many had to undergo a reorientation program before they would leave of their own free will. They were afraid to "enter the light."

So back to the paradox. I know that just coping with the day-to-day conditions of life can be enormously challenging, not to mention unforeseen events that can be traumatic. Believe me, I know; I'm on the journey too. At times our lives will be joyful and loving, and then in an instant we submit to guilt and fear and anger. Sometimes very minor things can upset our whole day, and quite unexpectedly a tragedy might even occur.

So what can we do? There are days when we might choose to hide in a closet until we discover that we take our problems in with us. Then what? Perhaps we might fall into depression or despair, or we just might pump up our courage and emerge in full ego bravado to set goals and timelines for success. We may set out to gain attention and importance. We may decide to go for broke, to become masters of all that we survey. But life never stays on an even plane. Sooner or later another up-set unfolds. How can we ever become a master?

What then is mastery? By the ego's standards – mastery is measured by success in the world. But we also know well that worldly success is fickle. People may even have personal up-sets and tragedies at the peak of apparent success. Sometimes life situations seem to be hopeless. Even rich and famous people commit suicide. Our lives, at best, always include ups and downs – ego reactions. This is part of life. Remember, <u>healing is a journey, not a destination</u>.

Journey Without A Distance

Riding the ox in search of the ox.

— Author unknown

Be Your Own Master

You are in charge of your journey. You are the master of your trip. No one can do it for you. Self-empowerment starts and ends with you. The choice to start the journey is up to you. Empowerment starts and ends with willingness, personal hon-esty, and responsibility, and leads to healing.

Be Your Own "Doctor"

We all carry within our souls the capacity to heal ourselves.

— Lewis Mehl-Madrona

You must be willing to take responsibility for you own "sickness" and for your own health to experience healing. By all means accept all the help you can get and seek treatment if treatment is needed. For example, if you are in pain, or if you are overwhelmed by guilt and fear and you can't sleep, you may need counseling or medication. If you have worrisome or acute bodily problems, seek appropriate professional care. See a physician or see a psychologist if you need that type of help. We need all the qualified help we can get. Treatment and healing are complimentary: treatment can facilitate healing; healing makes treatment efficacious. But healing is an inside job. You are responsible for your own healing and health.

I like to point out that despite popular usage of the term "doctor" to denote a physician, the origin of the word doctor means "teacher." [4] I try to encourage this understanding because healing and health are essentially a teaching and learning process. Also, I feel that we have become too dependent on titles and authority, and as a result, we fail to take responsibility for our own thinking, healing, health, and well-being. In self-empowerment and healing, you must be willing to take full responsibility. Biomedicine focuses only on treatment. Be your own doctor (i.e., teacher)! Empower yourself! Seek within! Healing and health transcend biomedicine.

The Problem and The Solution

Some people suggest that guilt is the problem; others suggest that guilt is the solution. How can that be? Surely both cannot be correct. Before we can decide for ourselves which idea is correct, we must ask what is meant by guilt? Guilt is a judgment of condemnation, most commonly perceived as

---

[4]The word doctor is derived from the Latin word "docere" meaning to teach.

blame for wrongdoing, and that guilt warrants punishment. Punishment, of course, leads to pain and suffering or stress. Consequently, people tend to become very fearful if judged or condemned and perceive blame or guilt as a threat or attack. As a result, we generally deny accusation of blame and become very defensive.

People frequently perceive wrongdoing by one another in countless ways, not only for crimes and misdemeanors, but for misbehaviors and shortcomings in personal relationships. We are even inclined to perceive our disappointments as attacks, and are likely to counterattack with hurt feelings or in anger to make our perceived attacker feel guilty.

How do you feel and react when you are blamed for mistakes or when you feel falsely accused? Do you defend yourself or justify your behavior? Do you then feel vindicated or do you feel guilty? Can you see that what really matters is not how others may judge you, but rather what you believe about yourself? Guilt reduces to self-judgment, how you feel about yourself. Guilt is a self-fulfilling prophecy. Guilt is a judgment made by the mind that sentences you to suffer.

How many times have you observed situations, even given all the facts, in which guilt and innocence were perceived quite differently among various people? But how could this be? For example, any contradiction to the primary commandment, "Thou shalt not kill," clearly warrants a judgment of guilt. Yet how would you feel about a police officer who killed an attacker to protect an innocent victim? And how would you feel about the police officer if she/he failed to protect you or a loved one? Do we not give medals to our soldiers for killing enemies in a time of war? These apparent contradictions lead us to a very critical awareness. Guilt is a perception (an interpretation), not a fact.

This brings us back to our question: Is guilt the problem or the solution? Most people believe and perceive that guilt and punishment provide the solution to curb wrongdoing and to force people to obey the law. Yet ironically, despite stricter laws, our prisons are overcrowded to crisis levels. Other people believe and perceive that guilt is the problem, that people behave badly and hatefully to others because they feel guilty within themselves. This is not a simple matter.

On the one hand, feelings of guilt can be a self-punishing experience and can serve as a reminder to carefully evaluate one's thinking and behavior. On the other hand, guilt can be seen as the problem not the solution because people who feel guilty commonly anticipate and misperceive attack, and they counterattack, which they justify as a defense.

Thus, what really matters in the final analysis is how you perceive yourself and, consequently, how you perceive and respond or react to guilt. Think about it critically! If you experience yourself to be powerless, unworthy, or condemned, you will feel guilty and fearful, or unloved, and attack yourself and others. Conversely, if you experience yourself as whole and complete, if you experience yourself and others in perfect love, would you experience conflict, guilt, and stress? Would you be motivated to attack anyone? Can you see that both the problem and the solution are a matter of your own perception?

Recall from Chapter 2 that the ego mode of perception

is based on conflict, guilt, and fear that leads to stress and suffering or disease. Recall that ego continually perceives attacks upon itself that demand counterattacks justified in the name of defense. The ego mind is a fearful existence, and let us not underestimate the enormity of its fear. In fact, we can readily see that if we are threatened sufficiently, our guilt and fear may intensify into terror or anger, and even into hatred and rage. For example, some people are so threatened and fearful of snakes, so terrorized, that they "hate snakes" and kill them on sight. To the ego everyone and everything is a potential threat. As mentioned above, guilt is a self-fulfilling prophecy.

Also, recall from Chapter 3 that we discussed another mind or way of thinking, or a true-Self that perceives itself as whole and complete. The true-Self sees the ego as a delusion of alienation, guilt and fear, which it perceives as a call for help, a mistake and lesson to be learned. As indicated, guilt reduces to perception in which the problem can become the solution by releasing one's guilt through forgiveness and healing. Guilt can then be perceived as the problem and the awareness and release of guilt can be perceived as the solution.

Let me hasten to add that we must instill and maintain law and order in our world, and we must include force as necessary. There are and must be consequences for misconduct, and that is a necessary aspect of our learning. We must not overlook irresponsible behavior (e.g., crime and violence). Such misdeeds must be met with deliberate and consistent action. There is no chance for self-empowerment and healing in the absence of law and order. Public safety, health, and welfare must be assured and vigorously protected. Some people may be beyond rehabilitation or may simply refuse it. Regardless, appropriate action must be taken. However, if we look carefully, we can see that guilt is the cause of the problem, not the solution.

Some Working Principles

Willingness

> *If you step back for a moment and witness the choices you are making as you make those choices, then in just that act of witnessing, you take the whole process from the unconscious realm into the conscious realm.*
>
> — Deepak Chopra

The power of willingness is choice. You alone choose how you experience every situation because the facts and conditions of life have only the meaning we give them. You are the source of all of your experience, and your communication and relationships always mirror your state of mind. If you don't like the experience, choose again. All that is required is your willingness to change your mind. This requires ruthless compassion with your ego-mind. However appealing it may be, you must release the attacks of the ego-mind on others and yourself. All other principles depend on this first one because willingness is choice!

Honesty
 Are you willing to be honest with yourself? Must you

insist that someone or something else is the cause of your upsets, or will you simply, honestly, accept that you choose and cause your upsets yourself?

Responsibility

> *Circumstances are beyond the control of man;*
> *but his conduct is in his power.*
> — Benjamin Disraeli

Responsibility is the willingness to experience yourself as cause. Responsibility requires free and conscious choice; if you are not free to choose, you cannot be responsible. If you react unconsciously, you are not being responsible, for responsibility is creation, not reaction. You cannot feel guilty and also be responsible. Guilt leads to ego reactions. Responsibility leads to constructive decisions.

Unfortunately we often misuse the word responsibility to mean fault, blame, or praise. These are the ego's interpretations because the ego projects false cause. It is very easy to blame someone else for what you do or how you feel. Someone else is responsible; someone else is the cause. This is not a trivial matter. We actually have organized our thoughts and language to express false cause: "You made me mad." "My wife made me angry." "My husband hurt my feelings." If you are willing to accept that you cause your own feelings and experiences, then you can be responsible.

Responsibility is a very high level of personal growth and discovery. The amount of power that you experience over your life is directly dependent upon your willingness to be responsible. You can empower others as well as yourself, if you are willing to be responsible.

Integrity

Mae West, in the classic movie, *She Done Him Wrong*, said, "I used to be ashamed of my lifestyle." "Did you change it?" asked her friend. "No," she said, "I just stopped being ashamed." Are you willing to tell the truth about who you are and how you feel, and to say what is so for you? That is the beginning of integrity. The truth must be told for its own sake. You cannot use the truth for an ulterior motive, or it becomes the purpose for which it is used and not the truth. One can be **responsible** only by the **willingness** to tell the **truth**. You need not tell your inner fears and the story of your life if you choose not to, but as Shakespeare said:

> *This above all: to thine own self be true.*
> — Hamlet, Act I, Scene III

A hitchhiker told me an incredible story. He said he had played an extortion game with major corporations. The larceny involved was at a petty level: making false claims and pursuing them with the boldness and tenacity to get away with them. He came to realize, however, that this practice did not serve him. In considering his motivation, he realized that he did extortion for excitement, but he justified his behavior: "The corporations could afford it." He told me, after he

*discovered the truth of his behavior, that he has
learned a different principle, which creates even
more excitement. "If you want to create excitement in your life, start telling the truth about
how you think and feel."*

— Anonymous

In our discussion of cause and effect, a fundamental problem is to know the truth. We often betray ourselves with a chosen misperception that we value more highly than truth or freedom. Our ego is so sure of its misperception and projection of
false cause to preserve its righteousness that the truth is lost in
the ego's interpretation. We often hide the truth and justify our
decision. We use 'our truth' to prove our point of view, yet the
truth doesn't prove anything; it is simply what's so.

Intention

*Intention is not a fanciful wish or hope; it is revealed
through every expression.* Look at your behavior; what you do
is your intention. Is it your intention to have your communication work? Is it your **intention** to be **responsible**? Is it your
intention to know, to discover the truth? Is it your intention to
express your meaning, feelings, and ideas openly and honestly?
Is it your intention to understand the message, feelings and
ideas of others? Your intention is revealed in every situation.

We daily hear the pretense, "it was not my intention" to
attack or defend, but nothing is more obvious than covert
communication: "I don't want to burst your bubble but . . ." –
obviously the intention is to burst your bubble. Is it really your
intention to transform your life and your communication? If

not, then so-called good intentions are a cop out. We do exactly what we intend.

'How shall I serve?' With good heart, (and)
good intention.

— Kurt Kaltreider

Humor

Laughter is healing communication (dissociation from the ego). "If there is anything that makes me happy, it is being miserable." Because we can communicate successfully without humor, I list it as a principle of choice rather than necessity. I list it for the fun of it. Like other principles, humor can be used to attack, defend, or escape as well as to support communication. I suggest using humor to lighten the trip. True-Self expression is love and is naturally joyful, so don't take it so seriously. When we take miscommunications so seriously, we give them mass and reality. Notice how beautiful our relationships are until we decide to take them seriously. Then we become involved in analysis, judgment, anger, guilt, fear, and control. Laugh at your ego reactions. Taking them seriously is the first step to sickness and insanity. At some level, no matter what the circumstances, the worst miscommunication is simply a mistake. Good humor is the key to sanity and to healing and health.

Since everything is but an apparition (a passing
experience) perfect in being as it is (a lesson to be
learned), having nothing to do with good or bad,
acceptance or rejection, one may well burst out in
laughter.

— Translated from Long Chen Pa

Mary was planning to go to a meeting that somehow was evolving from organized chaos. The meeting was to be in Tucson and then at a later date was changed to Phoenix. Mary was very upset about the shift in plans and called the organizers to let them know about her feelings.

John was listening to her attack but only with partial awareness. He was also upset but about another matter. He had just canceled his membership in a church that he felt was biased against other religions, and he was writing a letter to tell the minister how he felt!

Then in a flash, he saw humor in it all. We constantly correct each other, saying, "Why don't you do it my way?" We become correctors correcting correctors. John burst out in laughter! Look for the humor in a situation if you want to lighten up.

I once read an incident about a woman going the wrong way on a one-way street. A traffic cop signaled her to stop and confronted her with his pencil and pad poised to write a ticket. She looked up, smiled, and as though he were going to take her order, said, "I'll have a hamburger with onions, French fries, and a coke." The officer burst into laughter (Barclay, *Laughter Unlimited*).

Forgiveness

We do not understand forgiveness. A friend of mine likes to shock people, so he frequently announces to groups in his church that "God does not forgive!" Then, after he witnesses his desired effect, he adds, "Because God does not condemn!" But people do condemn, for we see guilt in ourselves and others. Thus people must learn to forgive themselves for their own condemnation.

Who is it who suffers from your unforgiveness? Our first attack is always upon ourselves. When we condemn another, we suffer. We all make mistakes and we must be accountable, but mistakes are learning experiences. "But it was done intentionally," you say. Then the mistake was one of intention, a reaction to a situation. Might you have erred yourself? Forgive yourself for having judged another.

I have a favorite story I like to use as an example:

Two young men of India went off to seek enlightenment and study with a master. One of the young men became upset with the other and went to seek the master's counsel. He accused his friend of wrongdoing and dishonesty, to which the master inquired, "Who did wrong?" The young man responded, "Obviously, my friend did wrong." The master replied, "Then why are you upset?"

Guilt is a judgment made by your mind, which sentences you to suffer. Forgiveness of yourself or another is simply a release from judgment or interpretation. We can only judge our own feelings. When you judge the motivation of others, you suffer the effects of your own judgment. If you decide that someone has attacked, used, deceived, or deserted you, you respond as if someone actually had done so.

The only cure for miscommunication and misunderstanding is forgiveness. When you try to unravel miscommunication to determine cause and effect, you are caught in the ego's trap. Your ego voice disguised in its self-endowed halo of righteousness will judge who did right and who did wrong and determine the guilty party. In arrogance the ego may submit, "You did wrong but I forgive you." Ego's forgiveness is censorious. It condemns in the name of forgiveness so it can demand its vengeance. The ego uses guilt as an attempt to control the object of its fear. But who in the name of sanity would choose fear, anger, and guilt when forgiveness can be chosen?

Forgiveness can occur only by releasing judgment and by compassion for oneself. This is love expressed. It requires courage to tell the truth and to be responsible for your own perception and your own condemnation of yourself and others. It appears so hard to change your mind, yet it can be done in an instant. Forgiveness is the only ultimate resolution for freedom and for peace. Forgive yourself for having judged or condemned yourself or another. You don't have to forgive, but you will feel better if you do. The choice is yours!

If you adhere to these principles, you will reach a bottom line discovery:

Arrogance: The belief that you control another's behavior, happiness, or well-being.

Impotence: The belief that others control your behavior, happiness, or well-being.

Power: The knowledge that you control your own behavior, happiness, or well-being.

If you are afraid of being hurt or hurting others, you cannot discover and express who you are. A master is empowered by his consideration alone.

True-Self Revisited

*The only way to be happy in this world is
to know who you are.*
— Valerie A. Skinner

*We shall not cease from exploration
And the end of all our exploring
Will be to arrive where we started
And know the place for the first time.*
— from Little Gidding
Four Quartets by T.S. Eliot

As you choose and learn to release your ego judgments through *true forgiveness* (i.e., releasing your *own* condemnation of yourself and others), you can rediscover your true-Self as unconditional peace and love. Through this process, we can also realize that Self-expression is true forgiveness and the key to mental and spiritual healing. As we empower and heal ourselves through true forgiveness, we extend mental and spiritual healing to others.

We can now place the story of the hundredth monkey in a marvelous and expansive perspective. As we choose to practice the process of true forgiveness for ourselves (by analogy, washing the "grit from our true Selves"), we learn and teach forgiveness to others. However, no one can choose forgiveness for another; each must choose forgiveness for one's self.

The more we learn to release our ego judgments, the more we release our egocentric identity (false self), and the more we discover and realize our true-Self as the experience of unconditional peace, joy, and love. When one rediscovers – revisits – and recognizes oneself as perfect love, then one re-discovers and knows others (beyond the ego) as perfect love. In other words, when we rediscover the true-Self – perfect love – in ourselves, we can recognize the true-Self – perfect love – in others. In this unconditioned state of mind (i.e., the natural mind), the mind is fully conscious and unified: it is aware of itself both as cause and as effect (i.e., the cause of its own experience).

> *Stop searching and learn to give your love.*
> — from *Siddhartha* by Herman Hesse

Self-love arises by feeling whole and complete within yourself. You cannot give what you do not have. We have forgotten how to extend our love. We have become confused by the ego's trappings and have found fear and separation instead. We have limited our love and power and expression. We extend ourselves only to a 'special' few for the ego's purpose, but we can transcend these barriers and express our true-Self fully to all humanity and to the universe and all its creations.

> *A human being is a part of the whole, called by us the "Universe," a part limited in time and space. He experiences himself, his thoughts and feelings as something separated from the rest – a kind of optical illusion of his consciousness. This delusion is a kind of prison for us, restricting us to our personal desires and to affection for a few persons nearest to us. Our task must be to free*

ourselves from the prison by widening our circle
of compassion to embrace all living creatures and
the whole of nature in its beauty. Nobody is able
to achieve this completely, but the striving for
such achievement is in itself a part of the libera-
tion and a foundation for inner security.

— Albert Einstein (cited in Kafatos)

We are often inclined to think that we have
exhausted the various natural forms of love with
a man's love for his wife, his children, his friends
and, to a certain extent, for his country. Yet
precisely the most fundamental form of passion is
missing from the list, the one which, under the
pressure of an involuting universe, precipitates
the elements one upon the other in the whole-
cosmic affinity and, hence, cosmic sense. A
universal love is not only psychologically possible;
it is the only complete and final way in which we
are able to love.

— Teilhard de Chardin

This realization transforms entirely the context, the expression, the experience, and the reality of life. Mental and
spiritual healing is full acceptance of oneself and others as
unique, yet united beings who are but parts of the whole called
humanity. This is the reality of unity – at-oneness with all
others. Indeed, the purpose of communication is to release our
ego sense of separation and to accept that we – our

true-Self – are already one. The experience of self-empowerment is oneness and healing, joy and love.

When I don't know who I am, I serve you.
(We teach one another.)
When I know who I am, I am you. (We are one).

— Translated from Long Chen Pa

*I may not know your name or recognize
your face, but I know who you are, and
I love you.*

— Paul Skinner

Chapter Nine Insights
A Transformative Vision

Describe how you might experience a personal transformation in your life. Make reference to the following points:

a. Through your communication

b. Through your relationships

c. Through forgiveness and healing
   1. You cannot heal anyone but yourself
   2. Healing yourself extends healing to others

d. Healing is a journey not a destination

EPILOGUE

You Don't Have To Do It The Hard Way!

I didn't get involved in empowerment and mental and spiritual healing simply from intellectual curiosity or out of my background and interests in experimental psychology and cognitive-behavioral sciences. Instead, it was the other way around. I became involved in these processes as a result of personal and family pain and suffering, and through a commitment that I and my wife, Valerie, have to find a better way of living.

Unfortunately, I have had to learn everything the hard way. My life is characterized in worldly standards by many successes, yet despite an apparently successful career, like many people, who may or may not admit it, I have encountered countless conflicts, guilt, and suffering over and over again. I had to hit bottom in some personal and health crises in my family, and finally in my relationship with myself, before I discovered the profound ego conditioning, conflict, guilt, fear, and insecurity that existed in me and that I manifested in all aspects of my life. Only then was I able and willing to fully recognize and manifest a better way. Believe me, it has not been an easy trip!

By allowing the emergence of new attitudes, we develop the understanding that life's threats are better dealt with as challenges.
— Joan Borysenko

Perhaps you are proceeding through life as I did without fully recognizing your profoundly conditioned egocentricity, and you have yet to discover that your pain and suffering in life are actually of your own making. Perhaps you are instead an enlightened being. Permit me to point out, however, that being enlightened in our egocentric world is extraordinarily challenging.

Regardless, you don't have to do it the hard way! You don't have to make the same mistakes over and over again until you finally hit bottom. This book is based on healing processes that you can learn and master through a conscious commitment and without undue guilt and fear, pain, and suffering. I hope to offer an alternative to you that can help you get on track without unnecessary searching and devastating experiences. I hope to spare you the need to learn the hard way.

Unless we learn to empower and heal ourselves, we have nothing that is of lasting value in our own lives and nothing of lasting value to teach or to share with others whom we love.

REFERENCES

A Course In Miracles. (1976). Tiburon, CA: Foundation For Inner
Peace.

Apollonaire, Guillaume. (1980). In: Marilyn Ferguson The Aquarian
Conspiracy. Los Angeles: J.P. Tarcher

Ashby, Hal (Director). (1979). Being There [Film].

Attenborough, Richard (Director). (1982). Gandhi [Film].

Arndt, Jr., William B. (1974). Theories of Personality. New York:
MacMillan.

Bach, Richard. (1977). Illusions. New York: Dell Publishing Co.

Borysenko, Joan. (1997). The Ways of the Mystic. Carlsbad, CA: Hay
House, Inc.

Borysenko, Joan. (1987). Minding the Body, Mending the Mind.
Reading, MA: Addison-Wesley Publishing Company, Inc.

Carnegie, Dale. (1936). In: Robinson, James Harvey. The Mind in
Making. "Dale Carnegie". New York: Simon and Schuster.

Chopra, Deepak. (1994). The Seven Spiritual Laws of Success. San
Rafael, CA: Amber-Allen Publishing & New World Library.

Clavell, James. (1975). Shogun. New York: Dell Publishing Co.

de Chardin, Teilhard. (1975). The Phenomenon of Man. New York:
Harper and Row.

Donne, John. (1624). "Meditation XVII" in: Devotions upon
emergent occasions. London: Printed for Thomas Iones.

Dyer, Wayne W. (1997). Manifest Your Destiny. New York:
HarperCollins Publishers, Inc.

Emery, Stewart. (1978). Actualizations. New York: Dolphin Books.

Eliot, T.S. (1942). Little Gidding. London: Faber & Faber.

Ferguson, Marilyn. (1980). The Aquarian Conspiracy. Los Angeles:
J. P. Tarcher, Inc.

Frankl, Victor E. (1963). Man's Search for Meaning. New York: Pocket Books.

Fromm, Erich. (1956). The Art of Loving. New York: Harper and Brothers.

Gibran, Kahlil. (1923). The Prophet. New York: Alfred A. Knopf, Inc.

Ginott, Haim. (1965). Between Parent and Child. New York: Avon Books.

Haskin, Byron (Director). (1950). Treasure Island [Film]. Disney.

Hampden-Turner, Charles. (1981). Numerous Schemes of Mind appear in Maps of The Mind. New York: MacMillan Publishing Co.

Heilig, G. S. (1980). In: Marilyn Ferguson Aquarian Conspiracy. Los Angeles: J. P. Tarcher.

Hesse, Herman. (1951). Siddhartha. (H. Rosner, Trans.). New York: A New Directions Book. (Original work published in 1922)

Holmes, Ernest. (1938). The Science of Mind. New York: Dodd, Mead & Co.

Jampolsky, Gerald. (1979). Love Is Letting Go of Fear. Millbrae, CA: Celestial Arts.

Johnson, Wendell. (1959). Your Most Enchanted Listener. New York: Harper and Row.

Jourard, Sidney M. (1971). The Transparent Self. New York: D. Van Nostrand Company.

Jung, Carl G. (Ed.). (1964). Man and His Symbols. New York: Dell Publishing Co., Inc.

Kafatos, Minas, and Robert Nadeau. (1990). The Conscious Universe. New York: Springer-Verlag

Kaltreider, Kurt. (1998). American Indian Prophecies. Carlsbad, CA: Hay House, Inc.

Keyes, Jr., Ken. (1982). The Hundredth Monkey. St. Mary, KY: Vision Books.

Korzybski, Alfred. (1973). Science and Sanity. Lakeville, CT: The International Non-Aristotelian Library Publishing Co.

Kosinski, Jerzy. (1970). Being There. New York: Bantam Books.

Lean, David (Director). (1957). The Bridge on the River Kwai. [Film].

Long Chen Pa. The Natural Freedom of Mind.

Mehabrian, Albert. (1975). "Communication Without Words" in: Speech Communication, Richard L. Weaver, II (ed.). Columbus: Collegiate Publishing, Inc.

Mehl-Madrona, Lewis. (1997). Coyote Medicine. New York: A Fireside Book. (Simon & Schuster, Inc.).

Myss, Caroline. (1996). Anatomy of the Spirit. New York: Harmony Books, a division of Crown Publishers, Inc.

O'Regan, Brendan, and Caryle Hirshberg. (1993). Spontaneous Remission: An Annotated Bibliography. The Institute of Noetic Science.

Paulus, Trina. (1972). Hope for the Flowers. New York: Paulist Press, A Newman Book.

Piaget, Jean (1959). The Language and Thought of the Child. London: Routledge & Kegan Paul; New York: Humanities Press.

Powell, John. (1978). "Dealing With Our Emotions" in: Speech Communication. Richard L. Weaver (ed.). Columbus: Collegiate Publishing, Inc.

Prather, Hugh. (1968). Notes to Myself. New York: Bantam Books.

Remarque, Erich M. (1929). All Quiet on the Western Front. London: G.P. Putnam's Sons.

Rogers, Carl, and F.J. Roethsberger. (eds.). (1969). "Barriers and Gateways to Communication" in: Harvard Business Review on Human Relations.

Rosenberg, Marshall B. (1999). Nonviolent Communication: A Language of Compassion. Del Mar, CA: PuddleDancer Press.

Russell, Peter. (1995). The Global Brain Awakens. Palo Alto, CA: Global Brain, Inc.

Sherman, Lowell (Director). (1933). She Done Him Wrong [Film].

Simonton, O. Carl, Stephanie Mathews-Simonton, and James L. Creighton, (1978). Getting Well Again. New York: Bantam Books.

Skinner, Paul H. (1978). "Speech and Hearing in Communication", Chapter 1 in: Speech, Language and Hearing. P. Skinner and R. Shelton (eds.). Reading, MA: Addison-Wesley.

Skinner, Paul H. (1996). Illumination (Book II). (in press).

Socrates. In: Oxford Dictionary of Quotations. (1941). London: Oxford University Press.

Tart, Charles T. (ed.). (1997). Body Mind Spirit. Charlottesville, VA: Hampton Roads Publishing Company, Inc.

Topf, Mary Jo. Student

University of Illinois Film Center. Biofeedback: Yoga of the West. [Film].

Vygotsky, Lev Semenovich. (1962). Thought and Language. Cambridge, MA: M.I.T. Press.

Wilkenson, David. From a presentation.

Williams, David A. (1981). "Communication Through Lecture," The Hallie Maude Neff Wilcox 1981 Lecture in Communication Studies.

GLOSSARY

All definitions in this glossary are used in the context of self-empowerment.

Acceptance	acceptance of responsibility for your own experience and starting from nothing and looking to your intuitive voice to create a new reality
Acknowledgment	your power of creation and the power of choice
Concept	an idea or mental image about how something should be
Dissociation	assigning your behavior and the cause of it to an external source, that is independent from yourself as the source, the act, and the cause
Ego	the ego—a false self—is who you think you are, an identity about yourself that you developed out of uncertainty and fear without full awareness
Ego relationships	a bargain between partners based on the misperception that one's needs can only be fulfilled externally through another person. Such a relationship precludes the joy and freedom each person desires in a relationship
Guilt	a judgment made by your mind that sentences you to suffer
Introjection	the belief that you cause the feelings of others
Love	the experience of wholeness and oneness
Perception	the illusion of knowledge based on one's interpretation of events

Projection	assigning the cause of your experience to someone or something other than yourself
Relationship	the nature of acknowledgment determining one's experience of oneself and another
Split mind	the ego splits the mind and places it in conflict with itself
True-Self	your causal or conscious-self as distinct from the ego

INDEX

A

A Course in Miracles 1
acceptance 116
ACIM 82, 111, 123, 137, 179
ACIM = A Course in Miracles 31
acknowledgment 78
    power of 72
acts and pretenses 100, 101, 130
Actualizations 31, 154
Apollonaire, Guillaume 161
appropriateness 117
Arndt, Jr., William B. 12, 157
arrogance 203
attitudes
    in relationships 96

B

Bach, Richard 33
barriers 53, 93, 105, 106
    beyond 138
    judgments 106
Being Number One 165
Biofeedback: Yoga of the West 19
Borysenko, Joan 13, 173, 209
button pushers 104

C

Carnegie, Dale 44
cause and effect 21
choice 119
    conscious 197
Chopra, Deepak 17, 169, 196
Clavell, James 69
communicate
    awareness 57

M

manipulation 132
master
    be your own 191
Mehabrian, Albert 53
Mehl-Madrona, Lewis 29, 191
mental reality 17
miscommunication
    (guilt) 91
mistakes
    opportunities for learning 183
    seen as challenges 183
Myss, Caroline 71, 96, 140

N

need 131
Non-violent 181

O

O'Regan, Brendan, and Caryle Hirshberg 6

P

paradox 189, 190
Paulus, Trina 169
perception 55, 58, 75, 91, 112
    chosen creation 80
perfection 188
personal reality 13, 26
physical reality 19
Piaget, Jean 156
Powell, John 112
power 139, 203
power of choice 12, 25, 27
Prather, Hugh 144, 145
programmed 34
programming 157
projection 22, 71, 199
    the ego's 128
protecting others 134

R

S

T

ABOUT THE AUTHOR
Paul H. Skinner, Ph.D.

Paul Skinner's investigative journey has taken him from the fields of speech & hearing sciences and neurosciences to the field of causal consciousness as it relates to science, spirituality, healing, and health.

As a Professor and Department Head at the University of Arizona's Speech and Hearing Sciences Department for over a decade, Dr. Skinner pursued teaching and research in psychophysiology (mind-body), psychophysics (mind-matter), and quantitative methods. He achieved an international reputation through his research in computer analysis of the electrophysiology of the auditory sensory-neural system and the brain.

In 1983, as described in the book *VISION: The Search for a Spiritual Pathway,* Dr. Skinner's personal life experiences led him to a paradigm shift and a career change. He accepted an appointment as a Professor in Family and Community Medicine in the College of Medicine within the University of

Arizona. Currently, he is involved with research in mind and consciousness; lifestyle and behavioral health sciences; and spirituality, healing and health. Major federal funding and a significant grant from the Kellogg Foundation have helped to further expand his research and training activities.

His creative endeavors also include the development and teaching of several courses at the University of Arizona in Lifestyle and Behavioral Health, and the writing of related books and professional publications.

Responding to expanding public interest and demand, he has established major conferences and workshops for the general public and for health professionals in the areas of "Lifestyle and Behavioral Health" and "Spirituality, Healing, and Health."

In keeping with his teaching and research focus of self-empowerment and self-healing, Paul and his wife, Valerie, also spend personal time enjoying the outdoors, hiking through the mountains of Arizona, and following spiritual pursuits – bringing balance into all areas of their lives.

Become a Friend
of

Spirituality, Healing, & Health:

Please join us in keeping alive the important vision of this book by becoming a *Friend of Spirituality, Healing, & Health*. Your invaluable partnership as a *Friend* will help in our efforts to bring to a wider audience our shared vision of the integral relationship of spirituality, healing, and health.

Our ongoing program of *Spirituality, Healing, & Health* will include workshops, conferences, and correspondence courses; books, conference proceedings, and manuals; audio and visual learning materials. Through the development of a "Teaching of Teachers" program, interested and qualified *Friends* can learn to conduct private or community programs in spirituality, healing, and health.

Yes, I would like to become a
Friend of Spirituality, Healing, & Health.
Enclosed is my tax-deductible contribution.

Name _____

Address _____

City _____ State _____ Zip _____

Phone (w)(____) _____ (h)(____) _____

Fax (____) _____ Email _____

Amount enclosed $ _____

Please make checks payable to:
                              Univ. of Ariz. Foundation/Friends SH&H,
and mail to: Dr. Paul Skinner
                        Lifestyle & Behaviorial Health Unit
                        University of Arizona
                        1642 E. Helen Street
                        Tucson, AZ 85719
For more information or comments, call: (800) 845-4649